BUILDING WEALTH

in

Changing Times

Jan Somers

The laws relating to property investment are complex and constantly changing. Every effort has been made to ensure that this book is free from errors. No responsibility can be accepted by either the author or printer for any action taken by any persons or organisations, relating to material in this book. All persons should satisfy themselves independently as to the relevancy of the material to their own particular situation.

Published by:
Somerset Financial Services Pty Ltd
PO Box 615
Cleveland Qld. 4163.
Telephone: (07) 286 4368
Fax: (07) 821 2005

First Released September, 1994

Printed in Brisbane by Inprint Ltd
Distributed by Herron Book Distributors

Copyright 1994, J.B. Somers of Somerset Financial Services Pty Ltd
A.C.N. 058 152 337
National Library of Australia
Cataloguing-in-Publication Data.

ISBN 0 646 19200 0

Acknowledgement

I would like to thank my dear friend, partner and husband — Ian, for his continued support and enthusiasm. Thanks must also go to my wonderful, patient children, Will, Tom and Bonnie, and my loving mother, for enduring the countless hours while I was either physically or mentally absent writing this book.

About the Author

Today, Jan Somers is just your average millionaire housewife. Fifteen years ago she was just your average high school mathematics teacher, who left the blackboard behind to raise a young family. With her teaching career on hold, she took advantage of her time at home to pursue other interests, namely property investment.

Jan's interest in property can be traced back to 1972, when she and husband Ian bought their first house. Although they accumulated many investment properties over the following years, it was not something that was planned.

Constrained somewhat by the needs of three very young children, it was a time Jan used most productively to read and to learn. Introduced to a personal computer for the first time by programmer and husband Ian, she relished the opportunity to analyse investment property in depth, playing with the figures to her heart's content.

At first she had trouble believing what the computer kept telling her, but no matter which way she looked at it, the answer always came out the same: *residential property, properly financed and kept long term, was a wonderful investment!* Jan now had an insight into why the family had been able to achieve so much through investment in property in the past, on just average wages. As a result, Jan and Ian went on to buy many more investment properties and now have a multi-million dollar property portfolio.

Jan never did go back to teaching high-school mathematics. In 1989, with husband Ian, she established Somerset Financial Services Pty Ltd and now enjoys sharing her knowledge with others through her lectures, books, videos and computer software. Her first two books *Manual for Residential Property Investors* and *Building Wealth through Investment Property* were both best sellers, the latter becoming one of the top selling business books for 1992, with more than 100,000 copies being sold.

Her firm's Property Investment Analysis (PIA) computer programs have become industry standards, and are now used by thousands of investors, accountants, banks and real estate groups throughout Australia and New Zealand.

Jan's new book, *Building Wealth in Changing Times*, has two simple messages: first, that it's never been more important than now to do something to secure your financial future and secondly, that her simple recipe for success involving residential investment property is just as effective in the nineties as it was in the eighties.

Contents

INTRODUCTION

Why is it that the confidence of people is shattered so easily? Why do most of us prefer to put off positive action in favour of keeping the status quo? The answer is simple — negativity. A single thought, a sole act, or a simple word, can plant the seeds of doubt in one's mind. Negativity is so contagious and so powerful that it can cause total inaction.

It would appear that my earlier book, *Building Wealth through Investment Property,* was a catalyst for many thousands of Australians to take their first step towards financial security. The book offered a simple recipe for success, centred on borrowing to buy residential rental properties that ultimately provided a retirement income. Those who followed the recipe grew in wealth and confidence with the progression of time.

But with the nineties and the recession "we had to have" came low inflation and low interest rates, accompanied by high unemployment. This created the perfect breeding ground for that social disease that destroys confidence — negativity. The outbreak was so widespread that it infected every corner of our community. Newspapers made headlines with reports like "Low inflation takes the cream out of property investment", while financial observers were making comments such as "Negative gearing is dead". And property investors began to have serious doubts about the validity of the recipe for building wealth that I proposed in my book.

This new book spells out why the simple recipe for building wealth is just as valid today, as it was yesterday — as it will be tomorrow. Times may have changed, but the economic changes we have seen are cyclic. They are not a recent phenomenon, though for our financial commentators and economists, perhaps they are a recent discovery. Low inflation does NOT kill property as an investment and negative gearing is NOT dead! But negativity is certainly alive and well!

As we approach the 21st century, we are witnessing not only changes to the economy, but massive long-term structural changes in our society. Perhaps the biggest change is the ageing of our population and it is highly likely that this single factor will change forever the way we prepare for retirement. This new book explains why it is more important than ever before to start planning *immediately* for your own future retirement.

Above all, it is my hope to renew the confidence of those who have adopted the recipe and to convince others that they cannot afford to sit back and do nothing for their future. In the words of the immortal Bob Dylan:

You better start swimming or you'll sink like a stone, for the times they are a-changin'!

Summary

Part I
Retiring in Changing Times

The recent trend towards earlier retirement and longer life expectancy, coupled with an ageing population and greater retirement aspirations, is creating a four-way squeeze of gigantic proportions.

There will be more people, with more years in retirement, wanting more money from a national budget that is already bursting its seams. And with the majority of our current retirees already living in less than desirable conditions, things can only get worse in the future.

In days gone by, it was probably only those people who aspired to be wealthy who assumed total responsibility for their own retirement, but now, as I will show, it is of critical importance for *all*.

I start by using figures from the 1991 Census, which have only recently been published, and other Government publications, to examine the woeful incomes of our current retirees. Their situation is certainly nothing to aspire to and the frightening fact is that I am not just talking about a handful of retirees, but the majority.

And just in case you think the problem will go away, I will show you what will happen if you choose to do nothing. I discuss in detail, the strength, or should I say weakness, of the Government's safety nets. I show you why you had better be kind to your grandchildren if you expect to receive any semblance of an age pension in the future.

And what about the Superannuation Guarantee Charge (SGC)? I spell out for you in no uncertain terms why there are gross deficiencies in the scheme and show you that, though well intentioned, the SGC will provide you with little more than an income equivalent to the age pension.

Then we look at your own future retirement situation. Do you want to endure, rather than enjoy your retirement? I will show you how to work out how much you will need for a comfortable retirement and compare this to how much you have now. Then you will begin to understand why there is such an urgent need to take immediate action.

Part II
Investing in Changing Times

In Part II, I assume that you have decided to take responsibility for your own financial future and show you why long-term investment in residential property can be the basis for giving you an early, wealthy retirement, free from Government handouts.

But why not invest indirectly in managed funds or in cash or in shares? And why aren't all types of property suitable for building wealth? We'll look closely at all these alternatives so that you can see why median-priced residential property is the best investment vehicle for the average investor.

I explain in detail the term "median-price" and then go on to show you why, contrary to all the clichés, it is possible to achieve high returns with a low risk by investing in median-priced residential property. I will show you why this category of residential property is the only asset that can be safely borrowed against (or geared) to a very high level. Gearing, and in particular, negative gearing, is explained in detail and I demonstrate with an example why it is this gearing ability that not only enhances the returns, but makes investing in residential property so very affordable — even for average income earners.

We will follow a typical couple, Bill and Mary, through the steps of buying their first home, then their first investment property, and finally how they build a portfolio of investment properties, giving them a net worth of more than a million dollars in less than 10 years. The simple recipe I use here is the one described in my previous book *Building Wealth through Investment Property*, and I show you how and why it still works, despite the changing economic times.

We will see how Bill and Mary calculate their retirement needs in terms of the number of investment properties they have accumulated. Then we examine the many ways in which they can balance the debt on retirement to achieve the income they want.

We then go back to your own situation and, with a "retirement ready reckoner", show you how to equate your own retirement income needs to a particular number of investment properties.

Part III
Analysing the Changes

Part III looks at the effects of economic, Government and social change on investment in residential property. This in-depth analysis should allay the fears of the many investors who have been wondering whether investment in property is still worthwhile in times of change.

We look at why inflation must not be considered in isolation from the other economic factors that affect property, and establish a link between inflation, capital growth and interest rates. I counter the claims that low inflation takes the cream out of investing in property and explain in detail how the returns, negative gearing, and affordability of investment property are not affected by the level of inflation.

We also look at the possibility of the Government changing the tax laws and evaluate the effect that such changes might have on property investors. I discuss the likelihood of negative gearing being abolished, the effect of changes to the personal tax rates on property investors and whether or not there will be new "wealth taxes" on capital in the future.

Finally we look at the often forgotten factor in property investment — people. How does the psychology of people affect property investment? We look at the movement of people in and around the country and I will explain why some population growth figures can be misleading. We explore the prospect of tenants buying property, with the potential for a decline in the number of tenants looking to rent properties. Will the lower interest rates induce "would be" tenants to be first home buyers? And what about the property investors themselves? Is it likely that everyone will jump on the band wagon and go out and buy an investment property? After all, if investment in property is so good, why isn't everyone doing it? In a most interesting study, we look at why the number of property investors has remained relatively constant over the past few years.

To complete the picture, in the Appendix, I show you how to answer your own "what ifs" by introducing you to our company's computer program. Using examples, I discuss in detail some of the more common "what ifs" such as "What if the Vacancy Rate is High?" and "What if I Pay Too Much for the Property?". I believe that analysing the effect of possible changes is the only way to understand and become comfortable with property investment.

PART I

Retiring in Changing Times

1
Are You a Lemming?

Lemmings have gained a reputation for being cute, cuddly and yet suicidally stupid creatures. These small Arctic rodents band together every two or three years and migrate en masse. However, this mass exodus is no orderly romp in the park. It is a blind, unstoppable rampage through forests, and across lakes and rivers, often many kilometres wide. Gathering other lemmings along the way, they stop at nothing, and eventually plunge into the sea where they drown in their millions. The few who stay at home, avoiding the mass suicide, survive to start the cycle again.

There are many such instances of "herd mentality" within the animal kingdom. Sheep herding is a classic example, while locust plagues and bird migrations have both been well documented. Not all migrations end in self destruction, and many have a sound biological cause that enhances survival. However, animals have no choice and instinctively, rather than thinkingly, follow the herd no matter whether the results of their actions are positive or negative.

Human beings are no exception in displaying herd mentality. Social pressures demand that we look like everyone else, do what everyone else does, go where everyone else goes, and spend money like everyone else. Fashion, custom, average, habit, standard, tradition — these are the words that dictate the way we live in a world preoccupied with conformity. Conformity is comfortable. Martin Luther King Jr described conformity in the modern world as:

Where everyone seems to crave the anaesthetising security of being identified with the majority.

However, the gigantic chasm that is supposed to separate humans from the rest of the animal kingdom is intellect. Intellect, as opposed to animal instinct, is the power of the mind that enables humans to know, to reason and to understand. Intellect should enable us to decide when to, and when not to, follow the herd. We have the ability to make a choice based on the information we have at hand and our awareness of the implications of our actions — or inactions.

And if we *know* that there will be a cataclysmic end, such as following each other out to sea to drown, then we have the ability to decide whether to go, or not to go. As the humanitarian, commentator and author Haydn Sargent, MBE has said:

You have the power to choose.

Why then, if we have this power to choose, do we see the majority of Australians following in the footsteps of everyone else, and choosing an impoverished, undignified retirement, dependent on Government welfare?

The sad fact is that in a country as rich as Australia, almost 80% of the country's retired citizens are dependent on Government pensions, living, or should I say surviving, on an income of about $8,000 per year.

All of these people made a decision — a choice — either consciously or sub-consciously, to settle for this meagre lifestyle in their retirement. But what most didn't realise is that this choice was made very early in life when there was still time to do something about it — not the week before they turned 65 and started looking around to see what they could do with the money they didn't have. This choice was made when they were young and could choose whether to save or not, spend or not, or invest or not.

Why is it that most people choose to follow the herd, "live for today" and retire on Government handouts? Ignorance and apathy are two major factors. Most Australians are either unaware of their future retirement predicament or comfort themselves with a "she'll be right mate!" attitude.

In a recent survey of young people, only 12% expected to retire on a Government pension, yet the reality is that about 80% actually do. These young people were under the illusion that something would "turn up" to enable them to enjoy a wealthy retirement free of Government handouts. Perhaps they expect to inherit a fortune. Or maybe they expect to win the Lotto. Or perhaps they are currently high-income earners with an imported car, a luxury house, and all the trappings of wealth, and expect that the money will just continue to roll in after they retire.

But with almost 80% of people retiring on an average of just $8,000 per year, clearly the money doesn't continue to roll in. The American economist Samuelson (in *Financial Aspects of the United States Pension System*, 1987) pointed out that in the century before 1937, Americans were the richest people on earth, yet most still died broke and lived their declining years dependent on their children, on the State, or on charity.

Obviously these wealthy Americans did not hear the alarm bells ringing, nor did they see the writing on the wall as to what lay ahead for them in their retirement years. They chose to "live for today", unaware of their future predicament, and were comforted by the fact that everyone else was following suit — the lemming syndrome.

Australians today are no different. In our ignorance of what lies ahead for us in retirement, we blindly follow each other like lemmings, taking comfort in the fact that everyone else is "living for today" as well. We must keep up with the latest fashion in shoes, clothes, food, housing, cars and in fact everything and anything that gives us both a comfortable living and social prestige — however short-lived that might be.

What is the answer to this universal phenomenon of failing to prepare for the future? Is it possible to force people when they are young to choose differently from the rest and to plan for their retirement? In a recent report, "Retirement Income Perspectives" produced by the Economic Planning Advisory Council (EPAC), it was pointed out that:

Households are short-sighted in their life-time economic planning, and tend not to provide adequately for their retirement unless they are compelled, or given strong incentives to do so.

So apart from brute force with Big Brother standing over us, it seems as though we all need some strong incentives — perhaps some powerful information — to encourage us to make that choice and to begin planning for our retirement. Let me explain how information can act as an incentive and help us to avoid the lemming syndrome.

What would you do if you were asked to choose the clothes you wanted to wear to work next week? Too far away for you to be bothered to even think about? You'd probably do like most people do and decide on that very morning, or at best, on the night before. There's no urgency for a decision, is there? But if there was a very good reason why you had to make a decision well in advance, the chances are you would do it. What sort of information would force you to choose today, your clothes for the next week?

Suppose you were told that you were shifting to another house and that the removalists were coming the week before you had to move. You now have some important information that should force you to act. So you'd pick out and keep aside some good clothes for work for the next week. Wouldn't you? You couldn't afford to be apathetic, or you'd have nothing to wear. Obviously it's much easier to choose to act when you have some critical information that creates a pressing need.

Over the next few chapters, I will give you some powerful information that should force you to take responsibility for your own retirement.

First, I will show you just how many of today's retirees live on the bread line and how paltry their income is compared to their pre-retirement income. This information will truly frighten you. Next I will show you what lies ahead for you if you *choose* to do nothing. You will be shocked to discover just how fragile the Government's safety nets really are. But what about the Superannuation Guarantee Charge (SGC) I hear you say? Sorry, but the SGC is not the cure, as you will see. And finally, I will help you to examine your own situation and to work out how much you will need to allow you to enjoy the style of retirement you desire.

After reading the following chapters, you will no longer be blissfully ignorant of what lies ahead for you in your retirement. You will have enough information to help you choose not to follow the lemmings to a meagre retirement dependent on welfare. Conforming may be comfortable now, but it definitely will not be comfortable in the future unless you choose to do something about it now.

2
Retirement Today

Have you ever stopped to think about all the money that you will let slip through your fingers while you are working? Just consider if you earned $30,000 per year (in today's dollars) for 40 years — that's more than $1,200,000 (in today's dollars) earned in a lifetime! And what will you have to show for it when you retire?

Today's retirees certainly know what they have to show for 40 years of work — maybe their own house, an old car, and an age pension of $8,000 per year! For them, it's too late to go back and retrieve a handful of dollars from that one million they have earned. For them, just a handful of extra dollars would make their lives just that little bit more comfortable. But alas, for them, the chance has slipped away. Will this happen to you too?

Retirement should be exciting and enjoyable — not just an enduring time between the end of work and the end of life. However, for most of today's retirees, the last years of their lives are not the most exciting and enjoyable times they could be. It is not a time of carefree living without financial constraints. It is a time when their income drops drastically below pre-retirement levels, yet it's a time when they are least able to cope with the change. It is a time that most spend eking out a meagre existence with little money left over for luxuries. It is a time that is now a long time because people are living longer and retiring earlier. It is a time for reflection on what might have been.

In this chapter, we'll examine in detail the results of past inaction by today's retirees to see just what sort of existence they currently experience. Once you absorb the details of this sorry saga, you will begin to see the picture of what could lie ahead for you. But there is one very important difference. In future years, things can only get worse. The picture I will paint for you in the following pages of today's retirees is a picture at its best. With an ageing population, and little prospect for Governments to cope with the increasing numbers of people on the pension, let alone to be able to think about an increase in the pension, our future retirees — that's you — can only be worse off unless they take action for themselves.

Current Retirement Income

Perhaps you thought I was mistaken when I told you that the majority of Australians retire dependent on welfare of about $8,000 per year? Or perhaps you thought it applied to just a handful of hard luck retirees. No, I wasn't mistaken, and no, it doesn't apply to just a handful of retirees. The Australian Bureau of Statistics (ABS) estimated there were 2.36 million people of age-pension age in Australia in 1992. Of this group, 1.82 million persons (77%) received pensions from either the Department of Social Security (DSS) or the Department of Veterans Affairs (DVA). Most of these pensioners were paid at the maximum rate of about $8,000 per year for singles and about $13,800 per year for couples. But perhaps you were under the illusion that this is not the "norm" and that most people earn extra from other investments.

In a 1992 survey by the market research group Reark, conducted on behalf of the Department of Social Security, it was found that nearly 60% of all lump sum payments received by people from retirement savings such as superannuation, were less than $20,000. Obviously, the lump sums received were exceedingly small, and furthermore, as we'll see later, most of these lump sum benefits were not used to produce income. Instead, they were dispersed into areas other than investments, such as cars and holidays. So overall, most of our retirees have very little in the way of extras to supplement their pensions.

Figures from the 1991 Census confirm that the income levels of our current retirees are desperately low and that only a small percentage of people retire on a comfortable income, and an even smaller percentage retire wealthy. These figures will be discussed in the following pages in terms of both individual and married couples' incomes. But what is most frightening about these figures is that the higher retirement income levels quoted are probably an overstatement at this point in time. When the Census data was collected in 1991, interest rates were the highest ever recorded in Australia, with investment accounts earning more than 15% interest per annum. Since those retirees with any extra income rely heavily on interest bearing deposits, their incomes today, in 1994, are probably much less than the incomes described.

The Association of Independent Retirees, consisting of members who for the most part fund their own retirement from personal investments, confirmed this view. They estimated that their members' annual income had dropped by 25% between 1991 to 1994 as a result of falling interest rates. Bearing this in mind, let's have a look at the incomes received by both single retirees and married couples, so that you will see how so many receive so little.

Single Retirement Income

According to the 1991 Census, almost 80% of retired Australians over 65 years of age receive less than $12,000 per year, the median being just $8,000 per year. The table below gives the breakdown of these income levels. More than half (50.5%) live, sorry survive, on *less* than $8,000 per year, while 29.1% receive between $8,000 and $12,000 per year. A further 8.8% receive between $12,000 and $16,000 per year, 3.8% receive between $16,000 and $20,000, and so on. Amazingly, just 1.4% retire on $40,000 per year or more.

Incomes of Retired Individuals Aged Over 65

Retirement Income	Percentage
$3,000 - $8,000	50.5%
$8,000 - $12,000	29.1%
$12,000 - $16,000	8.8%
$16,000 - $20,000	3.8%
$20,000 - $25,000	3.0%
$25,000 - $30,000	1.7%
$30,000 - $40,000	1.6%
$40,000+	1.4%

Source: (ABS 1991 Census, Unpublished Data)

Joint Retirement Income

Married couples represent about 40% (ABS data) of retired households but are little better off than individuals. Their median income is $15,000 per year (ABS Survey of Income and Housing Costs and Amenities).

But perhaps you're thinking that $8,000 per year for an individual and $15,000 for a couple isn't too bad. Later in this chapter I'll show you how these levels of income buy no more than essentials. I'm sure you want to live more comfortably in retirement. Most people do. In a study prepared for the Department of Social Security by the market research group Brian Sweeney and Associates, only 1% of people in the survey said that they would be content with receiving *just* the age pension (but remember that about 80% actually do). By contrast, almost 70% of people in the survey stated that they would need a *minimum* income per couple of $30,000 per year (in today's dollars) to be comfortable in their retirement — double the current retirement income for a couple. Obviously, the income levels of our current retirees fall far short of the aspirations of our future retirees.

Current Retirement Income versus Pre-Retirement Income

Being comfortable in retirement is a prime concern to people, with the majority of them wanting to receive at least three quarters of their current income in retirement. On average, this meant that most couples required a retirement income of at least $30,000 per year. (Source: Brian Sweeney and Associates, 1992). However, the fact is that today, most people retire with an income that is far less than what they earned before they retired.

The graph on the opposite page, constructed from information supplied by the Australian Bureau of Statistics, shows the distribution of incomes for individuals who are currently in the workforce compared to those who are currently retired. For the average individual, retirement means a drop in income from the median wage of $30,000 per year to the median retirement income of just $8,000 per year — a drop of more than $20,000 per year. How would you like a $20,000 pay cut at a time when you are supposed to be enjoying yourself?

But be careful not to misinterpret this graph. Don't be fooled into thinking that those who are currently on a salaried income of $30,000 per year drop to $8,000 per year, while those now receiving $120,000 per year drop by a similar percentage to $35,000 per year. Current wages have very little to do with what income you will receive in retirement — it's all to do with *what you do* with *what you earn* while you are working.

It is quite possible for someone currently earning $120,000 per year in wages to drop to the pension income of $8,000 per year if they have made no provisions for their retirement. And it is equally possible for someone whose current wage is $25,000 per year to retire on $50,000 per year — or more — *if* they have saved and invested for their retirement.

For a couple where both partners work, the reduction of income on retirement is similar to that of single workers. Figures from the 1991 Census indicate that the median income for a family is $35,000 per year — usually made up of a major income earner and a part-time earner. For retired couples, the median retirement income is $15,000 per year — still a drop of $20,000 per year.

Moreover, all the above figures are based on median incomes and do not reflect the fact that the majority of people earn more in the years prior to their retirement because their earning capacity is greater towards the end of their career than at the beginning. This would mean that in reality, most people would suffer an even greater loss of income in retirement than that outlined above. No matter what way we look at it, on average, retirees suffer drastic reductions in income compared to their working days.

Retirement Income versus Pre-Retirement Income

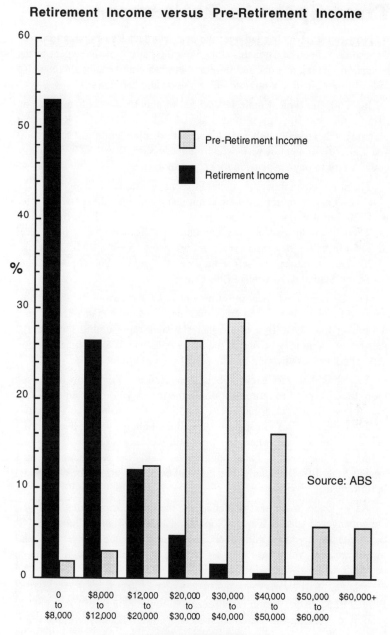

Income Brackets

Time Spent in Retirement

How times have changed over the past few decades. Figures from the Australian Bureau of Statistics show how the pattern of time spent in the education system, at work and in retirement has dramatically altered since 1960, bringing with it a mixture of both good and bad news.

In 1960, the typical male left school at age 15, worked in the same firm for the next 50 years, retired at age 65 and died at age 68. Retirement planning was virtually unheard of, and with death coming just three short years after retirement, it was virtually unnecessary, because Governments could afford to pay the pension for such a short time.

The story today, though, is quite different. Times have changed and the good news is that retirement now is not just a short-lived experience prior to death, but a major part of our lives. Today, in the 1990s, the typical male remains in the education system until he is aged 20, works for several different firms for the next 35 years, retires at age 55 and spends an average of 20 years in retirement before he dies at age 75. (Source: Australian Bureau of Statistics, Australian Life Tables)

The 20 years now spent in retirement is a far cry from the three short years of times gone by — in fact it has increased more than sixfold. And remember that these figures are just statistics representing the average Australian. You may be one of the lucky ones who live for much longer, and experience a retirement of almost half your life time!

You should be very excited about these figures. You'll now have even more time to spend in retirement doing the things you really enjoy doing. You'll have time to take that overseas holiday, time to play golf or bowls all day long, and time to catch up with all the hobbies you've been putting off for all those years when you were still working. This really is great news! The bad news is that although you'll enjoy the prospect of living a longer, fuller life, financially, you may not be able to afford the extra years in retirement.

As we'll see in the next two chapters, the age pension will soon be on the endangered species list, the Superannuation Guarantee Charge (SGC) won't guarantee you anything at all, and if you do decide to invest for your own retirement, you'll have even less time to accumulate enough money to be comfortable.

The bar chart on the opposite page, based on data from the Australian Bureau of Statistics, graphically reveals how the pattern of time spent in schooling, working and retirement has changed significantly over the years. It clearly shows how time spent in the workforce has been reduced, while time spent in retirement has been increased.

The Pattern of Changing Times

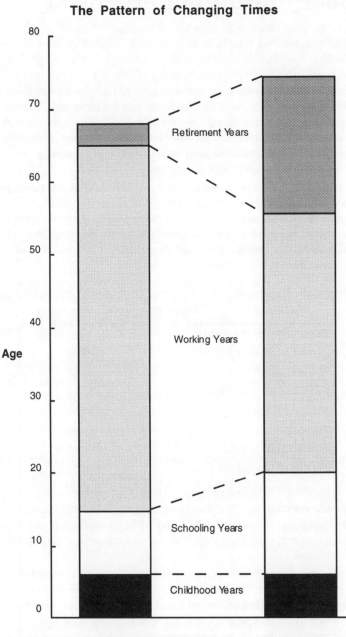

Money Spent in Retirement

In the past, when retirement lasted from age 65 to 68, most people probably didn't have time to think about how badly off they were. Death followed soon after the novelty of the gold watch had worn off, and the realisation that $8,000 per year (in today's dollars) didn't buy very much, barely had time to surface. But as you have just seen, the average retiree today must cope with living on $8,000 per year for more than 20 years — and possibly for much longer. Furthermore, today's retirees begin their retirement at a much earlier age, and consequently they are more likely to be capable of, and to want, a more active lifestyle in retirement. But this can be severely limited by lack of finances.

Perhaps if I spell out exactly how this money is spent by the average retiree, the reality of living such a meagre existence for such a long time might sink in. A recent report entitled "Income and expenditure profile of the elderly", prepared by Sanders and Matheson for the New South Wales Office on Ageing, described in detail the expenditure patterns of pensioners (see table below).

Average Expenditure Patterns of Elderly Households
(Includes Both Single and Joint Incomes)

Expenditure Category	Cost per week
Current housing costs	$26.80
Fuel and power	$8.10
Food, non-alcoholic beverages	$47.70
Alcoholic beverages	$4.60
Tobacco	$2.40
Clothing and footwear	$11.60
Household furnishings	$15.70
Household maintenance	$14.20
Medical care	$12.40
Transport	$24.20
Recreation, entertainment	$20.40
Personal care	$4.90
Miscellaneous extras	$7.60
TOTAL per WEEK	**$200.60**
TOTAL per YEAR	**Approx $10,000**

Source: NSW Office on Ageing, University of NSW

The average expenditure for retired households in the survey was just $10,000 per year. However, this related to households consisting of single persons as well as married couples. Hence, $10,000 per year is consistent with the ABS data discussed previously, where single incomes averaged $8,000 per year and married couples' incomes averaged $15,000 per year. Let's look closely at how the money was spent, so that you will see the difference between enduring and enjoying retirement.

Obviously these pensioners wouldn't starve. But $47.70 per week does not go far at the supermarket. And for those people who like a bottle of wine with dinner once a week — $4.60 barely buys the cheapest brand. Beer drinkers would have to be content with about four stubbies per week or two at the pub.

And transport? I don't see enough to buy a more modern car every few years. Do you know how much money is needed for that? The Royal Automobile Club estimates that it costs at least $180 per week to run a small car. A limit of $24.20 per week for transport is a long way short of what is needed. Or what about an overseas trip? The fares alone would cost more than $2,000 for each person.

And the grandchildren? Just imagine dividing the miscellaneous weekly allowance of $7.60 between several grandchildren. Are they really just miscellaneous extras? Or are they something special?

What if there were a need for "elective surgery"? Now we get into the serious stuff that really affects lifestyle. There may be a wait of several years, because ailments such as hip replacements are considered to be non-life threatening. Worse still, what if urgent surgery was needed — perhaps a heart by-pass operation? There are no guarantees that it would be done immediately in the public system and it is quite possible to die waiting in the queue. In this case I am talking not just about lifestyle — but life. Yes, it is possible to have medical insurance and avoid the queues, but even $12.40 per week would not cover one quarter of the cost of such insurance.

Are you beginning to see the picture? Do you think you would like to retire like this? By Third World standards, this expenditure pattern may be quite acceptable. But this is Australia — not a Third World country. And as rich as Australia might be, there is little likelihood that there will be any real increase in the $8,000 per year (in today's dollars). The next few chapters should enlighten your understanding of what lies ahead for you and convince you that things can only get worse unless you act now to prepare for your own retirement.

3
Be Kind to Your Grandchildren

Suppose you choose to do nothing about your future retirement. Do you believe that the Government will continue to look after you when you retire, just because it has "promised" to do so? Dr Blewett in his address to an EPAC seminar on the aged in 1992 "promised" that:

This Labor Government remains committed to maintaining the position of pensioners vis-a-vis those in the workforce by retaining the link between pension rates and average weekly earnings.

Promises, promises, ... Here's what the political journalist Paul Lyneham had to say about the politicians' philosophy on promises:

1. Never make a promise without an escape clause.
2. Never promise anything that has to be delivered before people are likely to have forgotten it.
3. Only make promises so vast or vague that you can never be held accountable.

Dr Blewett's intentions may have been honourable, but he tactfully avoided the word "promise". Using the word "committed" does not imply that there is any guarantee that pensions will be maintained at any level at all — *if* at all. So if you're thinking that the current level of pension would be OK if the worst came to the worst, you could be in for a rude shock. As I will clearly show you in the next few pages, the Government is in no position to guarantee you any pension at all in your retirement.

The reality is that the picture painted for you previously about today's retirees, is optimistic at best! Things can only get worse — unless you *choose* to do something for yourself. Why is it that things are so grim for future retirees? First, we'll look at the current national budget so that you can see why it is already bulging at the seams. Then we'll look at the factors that are adding budgetary pressures. Finally, we'll discuss why this budget is in danger of bursting, creating an uncomfortable situation for future retirees — *and* an intolerable situation for their grandchildren.

Our Bulging Budget

You don't have to be an economic genius to realise that Governments don't have a bottomless pit of money to distribute to all and sundry. They are limited by the funds they collect (mostly through taxes), which are then redistributed by the Treasurer via the Federal budget. The budget currently stands at $123 billion (1994/1995) and the chart below shows how these budget monies are divided.

1994/1995 Federal Budget

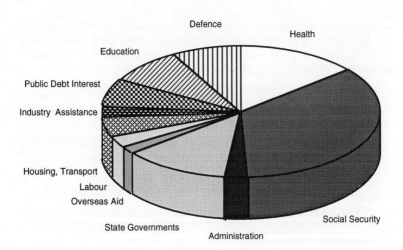

Of necessity, Governments are responsible for essential services, such as defence, transport and education. However, in the current budget, almost half was allocated to social security and health, with the aged being the major recipients. Certainly the disabled and less advantaged must be cared for by our Governments. However, the cost of looking after our ageing population is beginning to consume more and more of every budget dollar, with less and less left for other necessities. Something must give.

Even today, as I write this book, "things" are giving way. With the Government recognising that it can no longer afford to pay the eight billion dollar interest bill on the money they borrowed to pay for services in the past, they have decided to "sell off the farm" — namely the airports and Commonwealth Bank. What next?

Our Bursting Budget

The budget is already bulging with the pressure from current retirees. Let's look at some of the age-related factors that will create even further pressures on Government budgets in the future. This information should alert you to the urgency of the situation and should help you to *choose* to do something now about your own retirement, instead of relying on Government handouts that may or may not exist in the future.

Ageing Population

The projected greying of the population is perhaps the greatest single factor creating a crisis for future Governments. An ageing population does not mean that we are just getting old, but that *more* of us are getting old, creating a much higher proportion of older people in our society. This is a direct result of the baby-boomer generation born in the years following World War 2. The table below gives a breakdown of the age structure of our population over the next 40 years.

The Ageing of Our Population

Years	1991		2031	
	millions	(%)	millions	(%)
0 - 14	3.8	(22%)	4.7	(17%)
15 - 64	11.6	(67%)	16.7	(63%)
65 +	1.9	(11%)	5.2	(20%)
Total	**17.3**		**26.6**	

Source: Australian Bureau of Statistics

By the year 2031, more than 5.2 million people, or almost 20% of the population will be aged over 65. (It was 4% in 1921, and 11% in 1991.) Simultaneously, there will be declining proportions of young people (aged 0 to 14 years) and of those of working age (aged 15 to 64 years) within the population. To put this another way, the number of people aged over 65 will have increased by more than 173% (1.9 million to 5.2 million), while the number of *potential* workers will have increased by a mere 44% (11.6 million to 16.7 million).

Countries all over the world, and in particular many of the European states with socialist policies, are finding it increasingly difficult to fund pensions for their ageing populations. Australia is facing the same dire predicament, which it has yet to resolve.

Increased Life Expectancies

Healthier life styles and better medical technology have greatly extended the life expectancy of Australians, which, in turn, has increased the time period for pension dependency. Twenty years ago, a male aged 20 was expected to live to age 68. In contrast, today's 20 year-old male is expected to live to 75 years of age, and in another 20 years it will be more than 80. (Source: Australian Life Tables)

We are rapidly approaching Ben Gurion's prediction of many years ago, that the average life expectancy would reach 100 years of age. This is great news — or it should be. However, for Governments trying to balance national budgets, it is a statistical nightmare; and for individuals trying to balance household budgets, it is the killer of dreams.

Earlier Retirement Age

Another factor increasing the length of retirement has been the trend towards earlier retirement. Only 54.7% of people aged over 55 currently remain in the workforce compared to 85.8% in 1960. This in itself does not cause an immediate demand for the age pension. However, as we'll see later, double dipping means that people tend to spend their lump sums early in retirement, thereby qualifying for the age pension much sooner. It's all too easy for someone to spend a $150,000 lump sum at the rate of $30,000 per year for five years to maintain their previous living standards, and then resort to the pension when they run out of money.

Already there are indications that the Government is trying to reverse the trend to earlier retirement by forcing up the age at which women can receive the pension from 60 to 65 years, and likewise by increasing from 55 to 60 years the age at which superannuation benefits can be claimed.

Aged Health Costs

Total Government spending on each person aged over 65 is 3.7 times higher than those aged under 15, mainly because of health factors. (Source: EPAC report "Economic and Social Consequences of Australia's Ageing Population") With our ageing population, these costs will be even higher in the future, particularly as a result of the increasing numbers of people aged over 75. In a recent analysis by the Australian Institute of Health and Welfare, it was found that for those aged over 75, about half of the health expenditure was spent on the 13% who died within two years. As one observer put it, we are now facing those agonising ethical questions as to whether we wish to add "years to life" or "life to years".

EPAC have estimated that by the year 2051, the health bill for those aged over 65 will increase from the current level of around $29 billion to $126 billion (in today's dollars).

Double Dipping

Despite the fact that many people retire with superannuation benefits, most of them spend their lump sum payouts in order to maximise access to the age pension. Government policy does not require retirees to invest their superannuation payouts in income-producing investments, nor to spread their consumption over a number of years. We have all heard stories about the retirees who "get rid of" their lump sum superannuation payouts on swimming pools for their home, stereos for their cars, travel for their family and gifts for all their grandchildren, in order to reduce their assessable assets and in doing so, qualify for the pension. This widespread practice is called "double dipping" — first you dip into your lump sum superannuation, and, when it runs out, you dip into the pension.

A survey by Reark Research confirmed the observations that people had been making for years: superannuation payouts are mostly spent on areas other than income generation. The table below shows that only 26% of people reinvest their lump sums in either roll overs or other investments. The remainder spend it on anything from holidays to improving (short-term I might add) their general living standards.

Disbursement of Lump Sum Payouts

Main Use of Lump Sum	% of Retires
Roll Over	5
Other Investments	21
Pay Off Home	16
Clear Debts	4
Home Improvements	7
Holiday	7
Car	4
Gifts	1
General Living	17
Other	13
Unsure	5

Source: Reark Research for the Department of Social Security

Despite the trend towards greater participation in superannuation, there is no guarantee that this will reduce the numbers of people relying on the pension in future years. Double dipping is just as likely to happen in the future as it does now.

When the Bubble Bursts

How much longer can Governments afford to pay the welfare bill of our ageing population before the budget bubble bursts? Yes, over the years there should be an increase in the total size of the budget due to normal increases in the population, which in turn, should increase the tax base. However, there will be declining proportions of young people (age 0 to 14 years) and of those of working age (age 15 to 64 years) in the population. In fact, in 1991, the ratio of people of working age to people of retirement age was 6:1. But within 20 years, this ratio will have fallen to 3:1.

This diminishing proportion of workers compared to the elderly will be further exacerbated by the trend towards remaining in the education system for longer. For persons aged 15 to 19 years, the participation rate in the workforce has already fallen in the past decade from 60% to 53%, and is likely to fall even further in the future if employment opportunities for this age group continue to decline. (Source: ABS Social Indicators).

The lower participation rate by the young not only reduces Government revenue as a result of lost taxes but increases Government expenditure in the form of educational costs. As a result of these combined factors, any increase in the budget size in the future will in no way compensate for the disproportionate number of elderly.

In addition to the demands by future retirees, budgets in the future will also be under increased pressure as a result of many other claims. In the near future, both Federal and State Governments will be faced with funding the massive superannuation payouts that have been accruing to public servants. And since Australia is already over endowed with public servants (OECD has estimated that Australia has 20% more than other industrialised countries), these guaranteed payments will add even further pressure to our bursting budget. The Senate Select Committee on Superannuation described the situation as a "time bomb" with total unfunded liabilities estimated at more than $80 billion. Lewis and Boyd, in their book *Savings — Australia in Crisis?* ask the question:

Are unfunded liabilities a major crisis confronting Governments?

Obviously, future budgets will be squeezed from all directions. More demands by more retirees for much longer periods, increasing health costs, a dwindling tax base caused by proportionately fewer workers in the work-force, extravagant superannuation payouts to public servants, and an ever increasing interest bill on the public debt which pays for much of these costs. Governments have several options as to how they might balance future budgets. As I see it, here are just a few. Perhaps you could use your imagination to think up a few more.

Possible Changes to Future Budgets

Option 1. Reduce or Eliminate Age Pensions

One of the simplest options would be to drastically reduce or eliminate age pension payments to future retirees, while still maintaining essential services. This would probably create an outcry from those future retirees who have failed to act now. Nevertheless, it is happening in Canada where the Government can no longer afford to pay the huge social security bill.

Option 2. Eliminate Essential Government Services

Governments could maintain the pension in its current form but to the detriment of other Government services such as education and defence. But what a debacle this would create. Yes, the pensioners get paid, but at what cost to the general community? Would the country be worth living in?

Option 3. Borrow more Money

Of course, the Government could always borrow its way out of trouble. Governments are notorious for operating at a loss and have not hesitated in the past to borrow their shortfalls. Over the past 10 years, the public debt has grown from $9 billion to almost $200 billion, and the interest on this debt today is more than $8 billion. How much more can they borrow before the interest bill completely overwhelms the budget? Then what?

Option 4. Introduce a Special Pension Levy

As I have already pointed out, in the 1940s the Government of the day introduced a special pension levy, but it was absorbed into general taxes soon after. Again in the 1980s, the Government introduced a special levy called the Superannuation Guarantee Charge (SGC). However, as we'll see in the next chapter, there is a real danger that workers will not receive their intended dues.

Option 5. Increase the Taxes of Workers in the Future

Perhaps the most contentious option would be to increase the taxes of the workers of the future — your grandchildren. So if you, along with everyone else, choose to rely on the Government for a pension — you had better be kind to your grandchildren — they could be paying dearly for it. What a dilemma our future Governments face! Personally I believe that they will maintain the pension at a most basic level, paid for by the taxes of tomorrow's workers — your grandchildren — and there is every chance that they will rebel at the thought of paying these higher taxes. Paddy McGuinness, a well-respected newspaper columnist, also recognised the potential for a looming battle between generations. He is quoted in *The Australian*, February 26, 1994, as saying that the situation is:

> *... a recipe for generational warfare and social explosion.*

Age Pension — Right or Privilege?

Part of the problem we have in funding age pensions is that there is an expectation that has pervaded over the years that the pension will always be there and that it is a due right to all aged people. Today's pensioners are not entirely to blame for this myth. For the past century, Australian Governments have actively promoted the idea that they will look after older people in their retirement years.

From as early as 1905, Governments have discussed the possibility of establishing retirement income schemes of one sort or another. Between 1913 and 1939, three unsuccessful attempts were made by the conservative parties to introduce a NERRIS (National Employment Related Retirement Income Scheme), but they were always blocked by the Labor Party of the day, who believed that such retirement schemes would be heavily weighted against lower income earners.

Success was finally achieved in 1945, with the introduction of a Social Services Contribution by the then Labor Government. This levy of between 2.5% and 7.5%, depending on income, was somewhat similar to today's Medicare Levy, and was intended to provide pensions to all workers on their retirement. At the time, it was absolutely clear that this was a separate and targeted tax, especially set up to fund the age pensions of future retirees. It even appeared as a separate statement on workers' pay slips. This special contribution tax lasted for only five years, when, in 1950, it was merged with the personal income tax rates.

Over the next three decades, the age pension was paid for from general revenue and was available to *all* retired aged persons — without an assets or an income test. It has only been since 1983, with budgets at bursting point and Governments realising that it is impossible to continue to fund *all* aged persons in their retirement, that a means test has been introduced.

It is not hard to understand why today's pensioners earnestly believe that the pension is their right, not a privilege. Most of these pensioners would have been in the prime of their working years in the post-war era, when they were subjected to the Social Services Contribution. They were also brought up in an era when the pension was not means tested and was generally available to everyone. These are the ones who are saying:

But I've paid taxes all my life — I'm owed the pension.

They can be excused for thinking this way. However, with an ageing population, increased life expectancies, increased health costs and earlier retirement ages, the fact is that neither the special contribution tax nor the taxes paid by that generation over a lifetime was ever going to be enough to fund their pension for such a length of time.

But what about today's young people? They are growing up in an era when there have been no such special taxes to fund future pensions. It has also become widely known that the pension of the future is to be targeted at specially disadvantaged aged people. And yet, many of this younger generation still firmly believe that age pensions are a right, not a privilege.

In research conducted by Sweeney and Associates for the Department of Social Security, questions on attitudes to responsibility for retirement were put to people still in the work force, or about to enter it (see the table below). The survey showed that while 56% of people disagreed with the philosophy that it was totally the Government's responsibility to provide for us in our old age, an alarming 32% agreed that it was. Furthermore, people were equally divided (44% in favour and 45% disagreeing) on the issue of whether or not paying taxes earned them the right to receive the age pension. It is obvious that old beliefs die hard.

Attitude to Government Responsibility for the Aged

	Agree	Disagree	No Opinion
It's the Government's responsibility to provide for us in our old age	32%	56%	13%
You pay taxes all your life so you should receive the pension	44%	45%	11%

Source: Prepared for the DSS by Brian Sweeney and Associates

Let me show you why the taxes paid by average workers throughout their lives would never adequately fund a future age pension. The reality is that an asset base of about $380,000 (as calculated by the Association of Independent Retirees) would be required to fund the pension for a couple and provide all the fringe benefits. (This is based on the assumption that 5% of the asset produces an indexed income of $19,000, which roughly equates to a pension of $13,800 for a couple, $3,000 in fringe benefits and $2,000 tax.) Likewise, for a single pensioner, an asset base of $220,000 producing $11,000 in income, would be needed to fund a single pension. (Comprised of $8,000 pension, $2,000 in fringe benefits and $1,000 tax.)

It is almost impossible for any average worker to have paid these huge amounts in taxes during their working life and to have those taxes devoted entirely to their own future pension. If an average worker on $30,000 per year paid today's dollar equivalent of $7,000 per year in taxes for 40 years, then the total tax paid would be only $280,000.

Yes, the taxes paid by the workers in the past might be close to paying for the cost of just one pension — perhaps their own — but who would then pay for all the other Government services? Who would pay for our defence, our hospitals, our education and so on? We pay taxes to fund many essential services — not just our own pension!

The fact is that in the past, Governments weren't too concerned about the level and availability of the age pension, knowing that there was a statistical time limit of just three years for payments. Today, however, Governments are very concerned by the multitude of factors that have "crept" up on them unnoticed and unaccounted for — the ageing of the population, increased life expectancies, aged health care, etc., which have resulted in the huge increases in costs of caring for the aged. In the future, these costs will probably be met by the taxes of the next generation — your grandchildren.

Are you prepared to lean back, rely on the pension, and let the young ones of tomorrow pay for it? Or are you prepared to lift your effort and become financially independent so that they will be spared the burdensome taxes that they may have to pay in the future. Are you a lifter or a leaner? Below is an excerpt from a poem by Ella Wheeler Wilcox, in which she could easily have been posing the challenge that confronts us today.

Lifting and Leaning

There are two kinds of people on earth today;
Just two kinds of people, no more, I say.
Not the sinner and saint, for it is well understood,
The good are half bad and the bad are half good.
The two kinds of people on earth I mean,
Are the people who lift, and the people who lean.

Wherever you go, you will find the earth's masses
Are always divided in just these two classes.

And, oddly enough, you will find too, I ween,
There's only one lifter to twenty who lean.
In which class are you? Are you easing the load
Of overtaxed lifters, who toil down the road?
Or are you a leaner, who lets others share
Your portion of labor, and worry and care?

4
SGC — Trick or Treat?

Remember the slogan on television a few years ago promoting the Government's Superannuation Guarantee Charge (SGC) scheme? The tune was catchy. The message was clear. It went something like this:

Super? What's Super?
Super's here for everybody right across the nation.
The 3% you're getting now provides a good foundation.
Any more than that and you'll have cause for celebration.
To plan for your retirement think of superannuation.

The Federal Government has at long last acknowledged that we are facing a crisis in the funding of our future retirees. With the existing age pension arrangements no longer sustainable, and voluntary savings being totally unreliable, they instigated a compulsory contributory scheme called the Superannuation Guarantee Charge (SGC).

Now I must preface this chapter by pointing out that I applaud the Government on its initiative in forcing all Australians to take much more responsibility for their own retirement. The intentions of the scheme are noble. However, I seriously question several elements of the scheme.

First, because of the way in which the SGC has been promoted to the public, there is a great danger that people will become complacent about their retirement needs, believing that the SGC will provide a pot of gold at the end of the rainbow. And secondly, there is a serious risk that the end benefits will be "lost".

To fully understand why the SGC is no cause for celebration, we must look more closely at all its implications. What exactly is it, or isn't it? And more importantly, what will it do for *you*? Is it a trick or a treat? Are you being tricked into forgoing wage rises in the expectation that the SGC will treat you to a wealthy retirement?

SGC — What is it?

National superannuation schemes had been discussed for years, but it was not until the mid-1980s that the trade union movement seized the opportunity to incorporate superannuation contributions into wage deals. The Government of the day, the Labor Party, decided to embrace the idea as a national strategy because it saw that such a scheme had all the ingredients necessary to solve several problems.

First, the Government saw it as a negotiating tool for settling further wage demands. They reasoned that if workers were prepared to forgo wage rises in lieu of superannuation contributions made on their behalf, this could have the effect of stemming inflation.

Secondly, the additional savings accumulating in the funds was seen as a way of stimulating the economy by building a huge wealth base that could be used to boost industry. This would have the flow-on effect of creating more jobs and reducing unemployment.

But thirdly, and most importantly, there was the potential to solve the problems arising from our ageing population. The Government finally recognised that it would not be able to cope with increasing demands on our pension system. Savings in Australia were at crisis point, with less than 5% of incomes being saved for future use. (Lewis and Boyd in their book *Savings — Australia in Crisis?* point out that savings are now at their lowest level for 30 years — in fact the net saving level is negative for only the fourth time this century.)

And so compulsory superannuation was seen as a mechanism for forcing Australians to save for their own retirement. The Government proceeded to legislate to make superannuation compulsory for the majority of employees from July 1, 1992. The level of these contributions was to be phased in over 10 years, beginning with a 3% employer contribution, and rising by July, 2002 to a total contribution of 12% (comprised of a 9% employer contribution and a 3% employee contribution).

These contributions are then invested on behalf of the employees, who can access the accrued benefits in the future when they retire. Where an employer provides less than the minimum level of superannuation support, they will be liable for a charge levied by the Tax Office. By name, this is the Superannuation Guarantee Charge.

Here then, we have a scheme that can potentially lower inflation, boost industry, lower unemployment, and provide Australians with a wealthy retirement. Sounds good, doesn't it? It seemed like a win-win situation all round. It not only kept the unions and the workers happy, but also the Government. So what's the catch?

SGC — What it isn't?

Let's make it quite clear that the SGC is not a road to a wealth. It was never intended to provide you with a retirement of luxury. It was intended to make average and below average income earners, who had no intention of planning their own retirement, help pay for their own pension. In other words, before the SGC, our Governments paid for you to be poor with the age pension. Now, you will be paying for yourself to be poor with your own pension created from the SGC.

For most people, the belief that the SGC will provide a handsome payout on retirement, is an illusion. Even if everything goes according to plan — and we'll see just how unlikely this is later in the chapter — for *very* low income earners, the level of income provided by the SGC will be so low that it will need to be substantially supplemented by the pension. For those on the average wage, the level of income provided by the SGC will still be appallingly low, and they will only qualify for a token age pension supplement.

Let's suppose you're the average worker earning approximately $30,000 per year, and together with your employer, you pay into the scheme. The table below shows you the total amount you will have accumulated in the fund for a particular time period — *if,* and I repeat, *if* all goes well.

If you are an exception to the rule and have regular employment for 40 years, you will have accumulated $208,521. If, however, like most people you swap jobs and start off earning less than the average wage, then you will have accumulated only $106,856. (These figures are in 1992 dollars.)

Estimated SGC Benefits for the Average Worker

Period	Regular Employment	Irregular Employment
10yrs	$19,921	$14,659
20yrs	$65,901	$43,960
30yrs	$127,418	$76,749
40yrs	$208,521	$106,856

Source: Paper presented in 1992 by Dr D. Kalisch, DSS, EPAC Seminar on "Economic and Social Consequences of Australia's Ageing Population"

[Assumptions: SGC contributions phased in as per legislated schedule; a 2% real rate of return (above inflation) on superannuation funds; no administrative charges; a 1.5 % real increase in wages (above inflation); tax of 15% deducted from contributions; tax of 12% on earnings (assuming imputation and other offsets); no tax on lump sums.]

So what do these figures mean to you in terms of the income you could receive in your retirement? The table below shows the income levels generated if the lump sum benefits accrued in the SGC (from the previous table) were invested in either an annuity, or some other form of investment that is indexed to inflation and produces a yield of 5% (before tax).

Income per Year from SGC Lump Sums

Period	Regular Employment	Irregular Employment
10yrs	$996	$733
20yrs	$3,295	$2,198
30yrs	$6,370	$3,837
40yrs	$10,426	$5,343

All incomes are in 1992 before-tax dollars

Let's look first at the *best case* scenario. The $208,521 you would accrue in the best possible situation, would produce an income for you of $10,426 per year (5% of $208,521). That's providing, of course, all goes well with the fund. Because you now have $208,521 in assets and an income of $10,426, you would now no longer qualify for the full age pension — just a small supplement of about $1,000 per year. This would give you a total retirement income of approximately $11,500 per year (made up of $10,500 in income from the SGC benefit and $1,000 from the age pension).

It's a bit like six of one and half a dozen of the other and the average worker will be little better off than had he relied solely on the age pension. (But remember that you can't afford to rely solely on the age pension in the future because it may not exist.) The Government, on the other hand, is certainly better off because they no longer have to fund pension payments from their shrinking budget.

Overall then, for the average worker paying into the scheme for 40 years, the SGC will provide an income of around 40% of pre-retirement income (40% of $30,000 is $12,000). These calculations are in line with the Treasury estimations of retirement income produced as a result of the SGC. In his statement "Security in Retirement", in 1992, the Treasurer John Dawkins claimed that the SGC:

... would allow a worker with 40 years of average weekly earnings (AWE) to retire on an income of at least 40% of AWE.

(AWE is Average Weekly Earnings, which in 1994 was about $600 per week or $30,000 per year)

Now remember, the statistics above describe the *best* case scenario for the average worker. However, they are not representative of the majority of people who remain in the education system for longer, start work later, retire earlier, and switch jobs frequently. This means that the average working life is closer to 30 years than 40 years. Also remember, the baby boomer generation is already 45 years of age, with less than 20 years left until they retire. Therefore it is not possible for them to be contributing for 40 years to the SGC scheme. So our *best* case scenario is certainly not our *average* case scenario. If we look at the *worst* case scenario you will then appreciate the difference between what may or may not happen.

For the worker who is in the scheme for only 10 years and has irregular employment, the lump sum benefit of $14,659 will produce an income of $733 per year — not per fortnight, nor per month, but per year. In this case, such a person would receive *all* of the age pension of approximately $8,000, bringing the total income per year to less than a meagre $9,000. Can you see now why you cannot afford to be complacent about your retirement? If you rely solely on the SGC, you will be bitterly disappointed at a time when it will be too late to do anything about it. The SGC will do nothing to alter the statistics in Chapter 2, where we noted that 80% of the population retire on an income of about $8,000 per year.

The level of contributions is far too low to provide anything but a replacement pension — one that you have saved for yourself! Now while I believe it is a good idea that all Australians pay for their own pension, it would be disastrous if people falsely believed that the SGC would provide a wealthy income for them in retirement. Dr David Knox, Professor of Actuarial Studies at the University of Melbourne, was also concerned that the level of contributions was far too low. He commented that:

... some actuarial studies showed that the 12% was not going to be enough if you allowed for people to retire early, if you allowed for periods of unemployment, if you allowed for people to stay in education longer.

Even the Government acknowledges that the level is too low. In his 1992 "Security in Retirement" statement Treasurer Dawkins said:

But a 12% compulsory savings rate is not high by comparison with those in force overseas and thus the framework established by this statement will allow future communities to come to a judgement about whether the appropriate retirement savings rate should be higher.

Some of the more successful Asian countries such as Japan and Singapore have the highest levels of superannuation contributions, with Singaporeans saving at a rate in excess of 40%. (Source: Security in Retirement) At this level, Australians might have some hope of looking forward to a more reasonable retirement — that's *if* all goes well.

A Typical Example of the SGC Benefits

It would be useful to make some comparisons between the age pension, the SGC benefit and the income that most people consider to be the minimum to retire on. Let's consider a typical case of a married couple receiving the median income for families of $35,000 per year.

Without the SGC, and supposing this couple had done nothing about investing for their future, this couple would receive the full age pension for a married couple of about $13,800 per year on retirement.

Enter the SGC. Suppose the husband is the major full-time earner and makes regular contributions to the SGC for 40 years and the wife is the part-time earner who is in and out of the workforce for 40 years and makes irregular payments to the SGC. On retirement, his SGC lump sum would be $208,521 and his wife's would be $106,856 (see the table on page 43).

These lump sum payouts would provide income of $10,426 and $5,343 respectively (see table on page 44), giving a total income on retirement of $15,769 per year from an asset base of $315,377. The size of the lump sums received and the incomes generated would negate any sizeable pension entitlements, which would be limited to about $1,500 per year. Taking into account the combined SGC income ($15,769) and small age pension supplement ($1,500), the retirement income received by this couple would be about $17,000 per year.

How does this compare with the income they will *need* in retirement? Remember that the Sweeney survey conducted on behalf of the DSS suggested that the income required for a comfortable retirement by most couples was $30,000 per year — almost double the $17,000 income they would receive from either the SGC benefit or the $13,800 they would receive from the age pension if they had done nothing at all.

The chart on the opposite page should make it clear to you that the income provided by the SGC will never enable you to have a comfortable retirement, and in fact, will provide you with little more than the age pension. This chart compares the retirement income from the age pension ($13,800), to that received from the SGC ($17,000), to the minimum income required by most couples ($30,000).

Peter Costello, the Deputy Leader of the Liberal Party, also agrees that the SGC will not provide a comfortable retirement and that it is really an age pension substitute. On the SBS program "The Cutting Edge", when referring to the SGC funds, he stated that they are funds:

... where you will never see a return because you will have your funds eaten up by administrative costs and if they get a return out of it, all that will do will eat into their pension entitlements.

Joint Retirement Income Required Compared to the Age Pension and the SGC

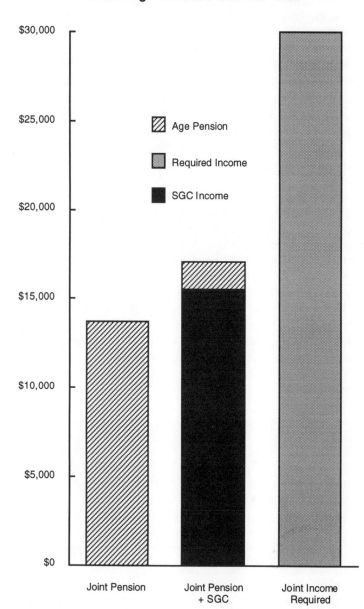

SGC — What can go Wrong?

It would be nice to believe that all Australians will receive their just dues from the SGC. It would be nice to believe that this world is perfect and that all the benefits from the SGC — as modest as they are — will at least be there to be collected in retirement. It would be nice to believe that the SGC will have truly solved all the budgetary woes of the Government. But as Dr Norman Zadeh said on the SBS program "The Cutting Edge":

The problem with pension funds (i.e. superannuation funds) *is that they are basically a gigantic IOU. You don't have the money now; they're supposed to pay you the money later; and between now and the time that you actually get your money, a lot of bad things could happen.*

The Government itself has recognised that there are risks, and has set up commissions (Insurance and Superannuation Commission), committees (Senate Select Committee on Superannuation), and made policy statements (Dawkins statement "New Prudential Arrangements for Superannuation") in an attempt to strengthen the security arrangements for superannuation. But despite all the powers, controls, audits, standards, committees, rules, restrictions, and regulations, these will never be enough to guarantee the benefits of the SGC. One of the Senate Select Committee's reports, "Safeguarding Super", drew attention to the fact that all the controls in the world do not guarantee that the benefits will be provided as intended. The report stated that:

There remains the possibility that even when such tight controls are implemented, some superannuation funds in the future might, as a consequence of poor management or fraud, not be able to deliver the retirement benefits promised to contributors.

The Committee also admitted that:

Since the publication of that report ("Safeguarding Super"), *the Committee has received many complaints of poor — even negative— fund earning rates, reinforcing the need for closer scrutiny of fund performance.*

And the Government's booklet "Retirement Income Perspectives", produced by EPAC, goes on to say that:

... risk lies squarely with the worker.

If you want to invest in superannuation *without* the risks, then you'd better become a politician. Their superannuation funds (which, by the way, are subsidised to the tune of 18% by the Government, sorry — us), are absolutely guaranteed. It seems as though the Government has one set of rules for themselves and another for us. So what are the risks that the rest of us face with the SGC? What are the "bad things" that can happen?

Privately Operated — Government Owned?

Although the SGC is a compulsory Government scheme, the funds will be managed privately by complying funds, such as the life offices, where they are ostensibly free from Government interference. However, many people have recognised that the temptation for Governments to put their sticky fingers into the pie is a real possibility. Hugh Morgan, the Managing Director of Western Mining Corp Holdings Ltd was quoted in the *Courier Mail* (November 2, 1993) as saying:

The big problem with superannuation is that because of the advantageous tax regime, Governments fall into the habit of believing those funds belong to them.

With the Government taking on a paternalistic role, and having "access" to a $400 billion pot of gold by the turn of the century, it would be very tempting to usurp its power to tamper with the taxes on the contributions, the earnings, and/or the lump sum benefits. It stands to reason that there is no need to make something attractive to encourage participation by people if participation is already compulsory.

Destination Undefined?

The SGC monies are directed into funds over which employees have no control. Not only do the workers have a lack of say in the destiny of the funds, but it is impossible for them to pull the money out and put it into a better performing fund. To get any money out of a particular fund, it is necessary to get special approval — and this is virtually impossible.

Questionable Management?

The superannuation funds are controlled by the trustees of the particular union involved. These trustees are appointed for their industrial relations expertise, not their financial nous and their reasons for selecting one fund manager over another must be questioned.

Fund Guarantee?

Although the SGC implies that there is a guarantee involved with the scheme, there is, in fact, no guarantee that you will receive anything in the end at all. The guarantee refers to the contributions, not the end benefits. In other words, it guarantees that you and your employer put money in, but does not guarantee that you get money out. Although the Government is strengthening super security with its reforms, some of the protection agencies such as the Insurance and Superannuation Commission do not have an encouraging track record of protecting the funds of the workers. Already we have seen some of these funds collapse in controversial circumstances. (*Sunday Sun*, June 26, 1994)

Unrealistic Time Frame?

The most generous calculations for the SGC are based on a person remaining regularly in the workforce for 40 years. But with a Government actively trying to keep people in the education system longer to ease the unemployment problem, and people pushing to retire earlier to enjoy life more, working for 40 years is a time frame from a bygone era. Moreover, at the time the SGC was introduced, most people had already been in the workforce for a good many years, and so their contributions would be considerably less than for a young person just starting work today.

Change in Government?

A change in Government could well see the implementation of a totally different policy. The non-Labor forces have made it clear that they wish to implement a retirement policy based on tax incentives rather than the current compulsory contributions. Peter Costello, the Deputy Leader of the Liberal Party has said on many occasions that he is an opponent of the scheme in its present form. A change in Government could see a complete overhaul of the SGC.

Lump Sum Benefits?

Although the SGC benefits can currently be taken as a lump sum, there are noisy undertones that could lead to the abolition of the lump sum payments in favour of indexed annuities — i.e. as a pension payment. The Government has already indicated that it wishes to encourage retirees to take their benefits as an income stream in the form of a pension, rather than as a lump sum. This would not only prevent double dipping but give the Government more control over the taxation of benefits. Legislation could make this a reality.

Boosting the Economy?

One of the arguments put forward for the instigation of the SGC, was that the monies invested would provide industry with much needed capital and boost the economy. This, in theory, would reduce our foreign debt by lowering our dependence on foreign capital. But as Dr Clarke, Senior Lecturer in Economic History at the University of NSW points out:

If you don't get good rates of return from investing the funds at home, they have to go offshore.

If the superannuation funds continually exercise their right to invest 20% of their funds offshore (as is currently allowed by the Government) this would be to the detriment of both Australian industry and the workers, thereby countering the philosophy that the funds will stimulate industry at home.

Preservation Age?

The age of preservation of superannuation benefits is currently in the process of being raised from 55 to 60 years of age and there is no guarantee that this won't be altered again as life expectancy continues to increase. Already, the Government has legislated to phase in the receipt of the age pension for women from 60 to 65. What next? Will you be waiting *ad infinitum* for a lump sum superannuation payment, which, remember, may not be a lump sum payment, but one that you are forced to take as an annuity when you are too old to enjoy it?

Amalgamation?

A rather frightening prospect is that any Government at any stage could abolish the SGC altogether, and redirect future payments away from the control of the superannuation companies and into their own coffers. Governments have a history of amalgamating special contribution taxes into general taxes. The precedent was set in 1950 when the Government of the day absorbed the Social Services Contribution into personal taxation. Who's to say it won't happen again?

Obviously, as Dr Norman Zadeh said of pension funds in general — *a lot of bad things could happen.*

Most PAYE workers will be forced to contribute to the SGC fund. However, to rely on it solely as a source of future retirement funds is pure folly. The SGC will *never* enable you to enjoy a comfortable retirement in the manner you would want. But since there's not much that you can do about the status quo, you will have to accept it and trust that it will add a few extra dollars to your retirement income that you have secured through other means.

5
Day of Reckoning

So what have you learned from the past few chapters. Were you aware that almost 80% of current retirees rely on Government handouts? Did you realise that the median income of these retirees.is just $8,000 per year? Were you aware that the Government may no longer be able to afford to pay the pensions of future retirees? And what about the SGC? Did you ever wonder just what it would guarantee?

It's all a bit frightening when we suddenly realise that the problems that we, as a nation, face in funding future retirees just won't disappear in the future, and moreover, will only get worse. It's even more frightening when we realise that responsibility for our retirement is now in our own laps. And unless there is a rude awakening across Australia, we will witness a nation of lemmings moving en masse towards a sea of welfare.

You can now see what will happen if you choose to do nothing. You can no longer afford to say "she'll be right mate", or put off retirement planning for a few more years. The longer you leave it, the greater the sacrifice. The choice is now yours.

The first step is to set a goal for your retirement. The easy part is to decide *when* you would like to retire. But it is a little more difficult to decide just how much you will need to allow you to enjoy a comfortable retirement for the entire time — not just enough to be comfortable for the first two years. As one financial observer has put it:

The only thing worse than dying is running out of money first.

I could also add another line to this little gem. The only thing worse than running out of money first is the *worry* of running out of money first. So how do you know if you will have enough funds to last for your entire retirement, or more importantly, enough funds to allow you to live comfortably in the way you desire for that entire time? Have you ever sat down to really think about it? Let's go through a few steps so that you can work out just how much income you will need for your retirement and whether or not you are in a position to retire today. I must warn you however, you may be in for a nasty shock.

Decide Your Retirement Income

First, you must decide on the income you'd like when you retire and whether or not it is for a single person or a couple. In deciding, remember that most couples want *a minimum* of $30,000 per year, (which is about $25,000 per year after tax) or about three quarters of the income they currently earn, whichever is the greater. So don't underestimate what you will need. But although you'll need more than you think, you may not need as much as someone else. You may not want to live in a large house or get a new car every three years. Only *you* can decide what you want.

The table opposite may help you prepare an after-tax budget. To give you a few pointers, I have included the budget of a pensioner's household for $10,000, one for $25,000 per year ($30,000 before tax), and also one for $50,000 ($60,000 before tax), just in case you have grand aspirations. The difference between the budgets is the amount allowed for the luxuries that make life just that little bit more comfortable — a more modern car every so often, gifts for your friends and family, travel if you feel like it; or simply assisting your family while you are alive to see them enjoy it.

What have you decided? $20,000, $40,000 or $60,000 per year, or more? Make a note of the *after-tax* income you would like when you retire and don't forget to make allowances for being a single person or a couple. (Note that these incomes are in today's dollars.)

Desired Income (after tax)   = $_____   (per year)

Now to get an idea of the before-tax income, a rough rule of thumb is to multiply the after-tax income by 1.2. This assumes that some of the gross income is tax advantaged.

Desired Income (before tax)   =   **Desired Income** (after tax) **x 1.2**

= $_____   (per year)

If you want more than just the pension, it must come from somewhere other than the Government. Where does it come from? Your employer? Probably not. Santa Claus? Definitely not. The fact is that this income is generated from the nest egg you have saved in your "piggy bank" over your working years. How big does this nest egg have to be to generate the income you desire? Most people's eyes light up when they see lump sums in the order of one or two hundred thousand dollars, so it might stagger you when you discover just how much you will actually need.

Budgeting for Retirement

Expenditure	Pension	Minimum	Wealthy	You
Essentials	$ per wk	$ per wk	$ per wk	$ per wk
Current housing costs	27	27	27	_____
Fuel and power	8	8	8	_____
Food, non-alcoholic beverages	48	48	48	_____
Alcoholic beverages	5	5	5	_____
Tobacco	2	2	2	_____
Clothing and footwear	12	12	12	_____
Household furnishings	16	16	16	_____
Household maintenance	14	14	14	_____
Medical care	12	12	12	_____
Transport	24	24	24	_____
Recreation, entertainment	20	20	20	_____
Personal care	5	5	5	_____
Miscellaneous extras	7	7	7	_____
Luxuries				_____
Gifts		5	30	_____
Luxury Food & Drinks		5	30	_____
New Clothes, Shoes		5	30	_____
Personal Beauty Care		5	30	_____
Carpets, Curtains, Paint		5	30	_____
Extras for Grandchildren		10	40	_____
Sporting, Musical, etc.		10	40	_____
Movies		10	40	_____
New Furniture		15	40	_____
Family Assistance		20	60	_____
Travel, Holidays		40	100	_____
Private Hospital Costs		40	50	_____
Dining Out		50	100	_____
New Car		80	180	_____
Total per week (after tax)	$200	$500	$1,000	_____
Total per year (after tax)	$10,000	$25,000	$50,000	_____
Total per year (before tax)	$10,000	$30,000	$60,000	_____

Estimate Your Future Nest Egg

Let's now convert your retirement income from the first step into a nest egg equivalent. We can use a formula to estimate the size of the nest egg you'll need to produce the retirement income that you desire.

Nest Egg   =   Desired Income (before tax) **X 20**

            = $_____

(Note: Both the nest egg and desired income are in today's dollars.)

Now let's make sure you have this calculation correct. If you would like a before-tax income of $30,000 per year ($25,000 after tax), you will need a nest egg of $600,000 ($30,000 times 20). What if you wanted a before-tax income $100,000 per year? Then you'd need a $2,000,000 nest egg and so on. Is this more than you ever imagined?

What is so magical about the number "20" used in estimating nest eggs from desired incomes? The basis is that an amount of money invested has two components of revenue — capital growth and income. This means that the investment will have a capital growth component to keep pace with inflation, and an income component that you can spend.

It shouldn't matter what the capital growth component is in exact figures, as long as it keeps pace with inflation, but the usual income figure is about 5% (before tax). Consequently, a nest egg of $1,000,000 would be expected to produce an initial income of $50,000 (5% of $1,000,000). Hence the reverse calculation: $1,000,000 nest egg = $50,000 income x 20

The multiplying figure of 20 is considered to be a reasonable indicator, but some investment advisors have suggested factors as high as 30 or 40. If you have been previously thinking in terms of six or seven times your Highest Average Salary (HAS), you should realise by now that it will be grossly inadequate. At first, it seems as though you will be receiving a nice tidy sum on retirement, but most people only realise how deficient it is on the day they retire when it's too late to do anything about it.

One further point on the use of the factor 20: this assumes that the capital base maintains its value throughout your retirement by keeping pace with inflation, and is not "eaten into" to provide income. This means that your longer life expectancy is catered for and you can also pass your assets on to your dependents. If you wish to have absolutely nothing left when you die, then you could use a factor of 15, which would provide the same income level, but only by dipping into the capital each time. But this is like betting that you will live for only 20 years after retirement.

Calculate Your Current Nest Egg

So now that you have a good idea of what you would like when you retire, let's look at the situation you are in now. What size nest egg do you have now? To do this calculation, you first need to estimate your net worth. What do you have to show for all those years at work? Add up the value of everything you own and subtract from it all that you owe — that's called net worth. The table below may help you calculate this.

What's Your Current Net Worth?

Assets	Value	Liabilities	Value
Own Home	_____	Home Mortgage	_____
Car	_____	Car Loans	_____
Boat	_____	Hire Purchase	_____
Furniture	_____	Furniture Loans	_____
Cash	_____	Credit Cards	_____
Superannuation	_____	Personal Loans	_____
Shares	_____	Leases	_____
Other Investments	_____	Investment Loans	_____
TOTAL	_____	**TOTAL**	_____

Net Worth   = Total Assets - Total Liabilities

= $_____

Although this figure represents your current net worth, it is not a true reflection of your current retirement nest egg. This is because it includes some assets that don't generate income for you when you retire. These assets include your home, boat, car, and any other personal belongings that you will need when you retire but which do not produce any income — not unless you want to sell up your home and furniture and live in a tent, and sell your car and ride a bike. So you need to subtract from your net worth the value of the home in which you'll retire, the furniture you wish to keep, the value of your car and boat, and anything else that won't generate income for you in your retirement.

Nest Egg Now = Net Worth Now - Retirement Home, Car, etc

= $_____

Could You Retire Today?

Now let's compare what you wanted for your retirement with what you have now. Is your current nest egg a bit on the low side? Perhaps totally inadequate? Did you think that you would have enough and now find that you won't?

If you've just come to the conclusion that you'll need a few hundred thousand dollars more for your retirement than you thought, and your current nest egg is about minus $5,000, you've hopefully realised that you need to take drastic action. And if it's of any consolation, you're not alone. When I do this exercise with the audience attending my seminars, most people come to the conclusion that their current nest egg is negative.

But don't despair. The purpose of this activity was not to discourage you, nor to deflate your ego, nor to send you into a panic. The main objective was to make you fully aware of your situation now, establish what your needs will be in retirement, and then help you set out a plan to get you there. In the following section, I do just this. I will show you a simple recipe for investing that will allow you to retire early *and* provide you with sufficient income to enable you to enjoy a more than comfortable retirement.

PART II

Investing in Changing Times

6.
Which Way to an Early, Wealthy Retirement?

You should now be fully aware of the meagre existence "enjoyed" by our current retirees. But with the demographic changes that are occurring in our society, things can only get worse for people retiring in the future. It should be obvious by now that you must take responsibility for your own retirement. But what should you do?

The first step is clear. If you *choose* to do nothing, you'll be relying on the age pension, if there is one, or the SGC, if it survives. You will spend your retirement years condemned to welfare. The alternative is to *choose* to do something by investing for your future, ensuring that you will be able to enjoy your retirement years, free of Government handouts, with dignity intact. The choice is now yours. Ignoring the situation or deferring the decision is the same as choosing to do nothing. Which of these paths will you follow?

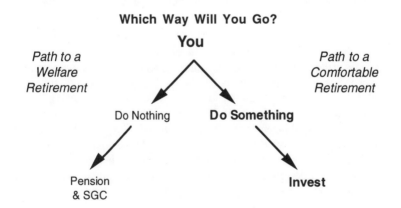

If you have decided to do nothing, go back to Chapter 1 and start again! Otherwise, read on! Having made the wise decision to do something is just the start of many decisions you are now faced with.

The Way to an Early, Wealthy Retirement

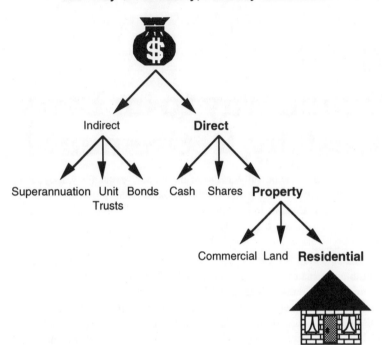

First, you will need to decide whether you will be prepared to hand over the responsibility for your future to a fund manager by investing indirectly, or whether you will be investing directly. Then, no matter which path you choose, you must decide on the area in which you want to invest.

Let's not beat about the bush. In the following chapters, I will be endeavouring to lead you through this financial maze to show you how investing in residential property can be the key to your successful, early retirement. The simple, do-it-yourself recipe involves borrowing to buy residential property to keep for the long term so that you can eventually retire on the rental income from the accumulated properties. By following this simple recipe, you will effectively be creating your own insurance fund, your own superannuation fund, and your own pension fund — but with one big difference. You will be able to retire much earlier, much wealthier, and with much more flexibility than by any other method.

But before I describe the reasons why residential property is the basic ingredient in the recipe, let's look at the reasons why I cannot recommend any of the alternatives with the same enthusiasm. Other investments are better than nothing, but in my view, fall well short of residential property.

Why Not Indirect Investments?

Having made a decision to do something and invest, the next decision is to choose whether to invest directly or indirectly. The indirect path leads to managed investments such as personal superannuation, unit trusts and bonds. People who choose the indirect option usually do so because they believe that they lack the time, knowledge or management skills to become successful investors on their own. Many also believe that they lack the funds necessary for direct investment.

However, as you'll see later, direct investment in residential property does not require special expertise (most people have a basic knowledge and understanding of residential property), does not dominate all of your time (do-it-yourself investments do not mean do-it-*all*-yourself), and does not cost an arm and a leg (it may cost less than $100 per week to buy a residential property worth more than $100,000, with *no* cash deposit).

Let's stop for a minute to think about why managed funds are called indirect investments. The name arises because the funds that are invested eventually end up in either cash, shares or property — the only three basic investments that exist. If a person invests in managed funds, they are thus indirectly investing in cash, shares or property.

You must understand that if you take this roundabout route, you pay for all the people on the roundabout. There are trustee companies and their associated staff, insurance companies with all their staff, administrators, fund managers, and sales people to name just a few, between you and your investment. You lose control of your investment and your returns are greatly reduced, because everyone along the route is skimming off some of the cream.

If you're thinking that fund managers are capable of making better investment decisions than you, then let me remind you of how many of them were caught out in the stock market crash of 1987 and the collapse of the commercial property market not long after. Yes, there are some very successful fund managers in the market place, but choosing the astute ones can be a nightmare. It is widely accepted that managed funds with a good track record suddenly drop in value if their good managers leave. This has happened several times in recent years so it would be important to watch the financial press to see who is going where. This in itself can be a daunting task and defeats the purpose of why people invest indirectly — and that is to be free of such decisions.

If nothing else, choosing managed investments is better than doing nothing. But farming out your profits to all and sundry along the indirect route may not allow you to achieve your goal of retiring early and wealthy.

Why Not Cash?

Of the direct investments, most people can relate to depositing money in a bank. But how many people do you know who have made enough money for a comfortable retirement by investing in cash in the bank? A few? None? It's more likely the case that you know someone with cash in the bank who *thinks* they have enough to retire on but in fact have been getting poorer and poorer each year.

Most people feel secure with cash in the bank. However, these people do not understand that the twin ravages of inflation and taxation make it very insecure. People who rely on interest from invested cash are in a no-win situation, no matter what the level of interest rates.

If interest rates are high, cash investors receive an "apparently" good income from the interest. However, taxation takes away up to half the income and furthermore, because high interest rates are usually coupled with high inflation, the value of both the income and the base capital is continually eroded, generating fewer and fewer "real" dollars in interest. With low interest rates, the income is a pittance. The only good news is that the tax is less and the capital devalues more slowly.

Possibly you are thinking, though, that it is only recently that cash investments have performed poorly. Let's take a look, then, at their track record over the past four decades. The chart on the opposite page tracks the inflation rate or Consumer Price Index (Source: Australian Bureau of Statistics), the interest rates or trading bank term deposit rate (Source: Reserve Bank) and the real rate of return, taking into account inflation at the time, and a 40% marginal tax rate. (This tax rate is conservative in view of the fact that in the 1950s and 60s, top marginal rates were 60+%.)

The dark line on the graph shows the percentage return after allowing for tax and inflation year by year and represents the *real* return on cash investments. For the most part, the real after-tax, after-inflation returns were negative, reaching a trough of minus 25% in the early 1950s and again at minus 12% in the mid-70s. Only in a few years was the return positive, and even then, at most 4%. Interestingly, this "high" return, was achieved in the early 90s, at a time when interest rates had dropped to their lowest levels for two decades, but were high relative to inflation.

Cash investments are clearly not your pathway to wealth and will never allow you to retire early and wealthy. However, if you think about it, investing in cash allows other people to retire early and wealthy. How? Because the bank is simply the "go-between", and for a nominal fee, simply borrows from you to lend to other people who wish to invest it in other more profitable areas so that they can retire earlier and wealthier!

After-Tax, After-Inflation Returns from Cash

% Return

Inflation
2yr Fixed Term Deposit Rate
After-Tax, After-Inflation Return

Source: ABS, Reserve Bank

Why Not Shares?

There is a noble philosophy behind investment in shares: invest in a company and you contribute to the country's economy, which in turn creates more jobs and boosts productivity. The spinoff is that when the company makes a lot of money, so do you. Sounds good, doesn't it? But the philosophy and the reality are light years apart.

The reality is that investing in shares is not a secure road to wealth. Yes, people *do* make money from shares. However, there are high risks attached, which lessen your chance of retiring early and wealthy. We need only look at the chart below to understand why these risks exist. It shows the yearly growth rates for the All Ordinaries Index between 1960 and 1994 and highlights the extreme volatility of the share market with the All Ords rising by up to 100% in one year and falling as much as 50% in others. In fact, growth rates were negative for about half the time. (Negative growth rates indicate a loss of capital and this occurs when the zero line is crossed.)

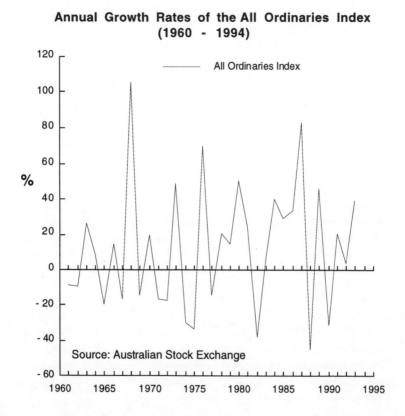

Annual Growth Rates of the All Ordinaries Index (1960 - 1994)

Source: Australian Stock Exchange

If these figures are compounded over many years, you can see (in the graph below) an upward trend of around 7% per year.

Shares Need Timing

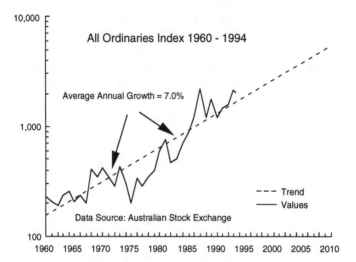

Notice how the actual values jump way above and below the trend line, indicating the extreme volatility in the market, even over the longer term. If you had bought at the wrong time, the long-term compound growth factor of 7% does not compensate for such severe fluctuations. In other words, timing is critical to share market investing, and picking "when to buy" and "when to sell" is a crucial element in success.

Furthermore, although there are some very successful companies, there are thousands of companies that are no longer in existence. We have short memories when it comes to Ariadne, Bond Corporation, Quintex, etc., etc. and ad infinitum. So not only is the share market a "when to" investment, but it is also a "which to" investment. Who was enough "in the know" a decade ago to be able to pick the winners and identify the losers? You need skill (or luck) to know which shares to invest in, and when many professional fund managers can't get it right, do you think you will fare any better?

Perhaps one of the greatest downsides of investing in shares is that, because of their high volatility, it is difficult, if not impossible, to gear (or borrow) against their value. And as I'll show you in the next chapter (see page 78), gearing is an important tool in compounding the returns from an investment, allowing you to build wealth more quickly.

Why Not All Types of Property?

You've just seen why managed investments, cash and shares may not be suitable as investments for your retirement. But what about property? Much confusion arises when the term "property" is bandied around so that when you read newspaper headlines such as "Property Prices Slump 40%" you really need to know exactly what type of property they are referring to.

Otherwise it's a bit like saying bread is good for you. Are all breads good for you? Or are some breads better than others? Obviously if we categorise bread into white or wholegrain, then we are in a better position to decide what is best.

Property, in a sense, is exactly the same. Are all types of property good for investment? Or are some types better than others? "Property" is an all encompassing word that takes in land (including vacant blocks and rural land), commercial property (including industrial and office buildings) and residential property — and even then, as we'll see later, there are categories. So we must clearly distinguish which type of property we are talking about before we can make any judgement.

Neither commercial property nor land is suitable as a vehicle for building wealth for the average investor. Let's have a brief look why.

Commercial Property

Allow me to make a statement about commercial property before I go into the reasons as to why it may not be as secure and sound as residential property for building wealth. It *is* possible to make money by investing in commercial property. Some of the benefits include the large capital gains that can be made in a short space of time, the high yields that can far exceed those of residential property, and the lower expenses because the tenant often pays for most of the on-going costs. Overall, commercial property has the *potential* to be a very sound investment.

However, this being said, there are many downsides that the average investor may have trouble coping with. Although there is the potential to make large capital gains, there is also the chance of making even larger capital losses. Commercial property is closely tied to the corporate and business sector and consequently it can be almost as volatile as the share market. As we have seen, especially in recent years, it does not have long term *steady* growth and many commercial properties have lately suffered substantial falls in value. Some have been sold for less than half their valued price at the peak of the markets in 1989. The fact that financial institutions usually only lend to 70% of the value of commercial property is further testament to its potential volatility.

Moreover, although there is the potential to receive high yields from commercial property, the vacancy factor associated with such property can be quite high, with capital cities experiencing vacancy rates of between 15% and 40% in recessionary times. In places like Sydney and Melbourne, one in three office blocks was vacant in 1992. These very high vacancy rates negate the potentially high rental yields. Yes, high yields of between 10% and 20% are attainable from commercial property, with the tenants paying many of the outgoings such as rates, insurance and maintenance. However, *potentially* high yields are of no use if the premises are vacant.

Contributing to the higher vacancy factor is the changing usage of commercial property, particularly offices and retail shops, brought about by the communications revolution. Technological advances have already, and will continue to transform the way in which both the business world and the ordinary citizen go about their daily affairs.

Offices in the Central Business District (CBD) have borne the brunt of this revolution with the advent of the personal computer being one of the main catalysts for the change. Not only have personal computers reduced the need for office workers, lessened the requirement for office space, and eliminated the necessity for offices to be centrally located, but they have enabled many people to set up a business at home. This "work from home" trend will continue to increase on an unprecedented scale, weakening the demand for commercial office space. An article in *Business Review Weekly*, June, 1994 said of the growing number of home businesses:

BIS Shrapnel estimates that 12% of Australian households, or 710,000, are involved in a home-based business, and that the figure is expected to be 16% within two years. In the United States, 37% of homes are used for running a business.

Another major technological advance that is in its teething stages, but which has the potential to change forever the way we shop, is interactive television. Canada has set the scene for massive changes in the future with the introduction of this new and exciting method of telecommunications. It has been predicted that within a decade, every Australian will be able to shop from home. Retail shops, as we know them today, may have all but disappeared.

Obviously, as a result of technological advances, commercial property is experiencing changing times. Yes, people can successfully invest in commercial property, but the average investor cannot be expected to have the experience necessary to identify the changing needs of commercial markets and cater accordingly. For a business operator, it represents an excellent opportunity to purchase their own premises, knowing that the tenant (that's themselves) has a viable and ongoing business.

Land

And land? Land can offer excellent growth, but unless it is income producing, your investment dollar is not working hard enough for you. The reason for this is that with no income, there are no tax concessions, and consequently, with no tenant and no tax benefits, you have to put in more of your own funds. For people borrowing to buy land, the non-tax deductibility of the interest bill makes it a very expensive exercise and consequently, land is not as affordable as income-producing property.

I have known many people who have bought land with a view to developing it and then find that they can't afford the million or so dollars needed to fulfil the potential of the land. Instead of reaping the rewards themselves, they usually find that they must on-sell to a professional developer, thereby passing on the real profits to someone else. And to top it off, they have to pay tax on any profits from the sale at marginal income tax rates, without any inflationary allowance.

Residential Property

Apart from food, shelter is one of our basic necessities, and in the following chapter I will show you why I consider residential property to be the vehicle best suited for building wealth for retirement for the average investor.

7
Why Median-Priced Residential Property?

In the previous chapter I devoted a lot of attention to "what not to do". Indirect investments may make the middlemen rich, but generally do not offer consistent high returns or enough control; cash is attacked on both sides by inflation and taxation; shares may be an exciting way to invest, but their volatility makes them a "which to, when to" type of investment; commercial property does not fare much better than shares in terms of volatility and usually requires a substantial outlay of capital; vacant land may be as solid as a rock, but it lacks the income and the tax advantages, making it less affordable.

In the next few chapters, I want to show you "what you can do" — and that is to invest in residential property; and why you should do it. But first, I should be a little more specific about the category of residential property I am referring to. Residential property represents the largest single asset market in Australia (valued at more than $700 billion) and properties come in all shapes, sizes, prices, and locations. Which one is best? The waterside mansion that you have always dreamed of living in may not be the most affordable investment, while at the other extreme, you would have difficulty renting out a cheap fibro shack under the railway bridge. So which category of residential property is the best vehicle for building wealth?

I advocate reasonably priced, reasonably located, and reasonably well presented residential property in regions with reasonable capital growth potential (any capital city or large provincial town). What do I mean by "reasonable"? Perhaps a more tangible guide to a "reasonable" investment property is a "median-priced" residential property. This term is a little confusing to many people, but since this is the closest description that I can provide of what represents a "reasonable" investment property, and since most of the published statistics relate to median-priced properties, I should first define the term "median price".

What is "Median Price"?

The term "median price" has a very specific meaning in property. It is:

The price at which half the properties sell for more and half sell for less.

It is also the most common index used for property prices because it is less distorted by the sale of a few high-priced properties. To help us better understand how "median price" is calculated, let's look at a specific market such as Sydney.

In producing the graph below, I have used data supplied by Residex, a Sydney-based actuarial company that has information relating to *every* residential property sold in the Sydney area over the past few decades. For example, a total of 9,342 properties were sold in Sydney in the December quarter of 1993 and prices ranged from a low of $50,000 to a high of more than $20,000,000. The individual sale prices of these properties, together with the number of sales at each price, are shown in the graph below. In this particular case, the median-price is $180,000, which is the price at which half the properties (4,671) sold for more than $180,000 and half (4,671) sold for less than $180,000.

Defining Median-Priced Residential Property

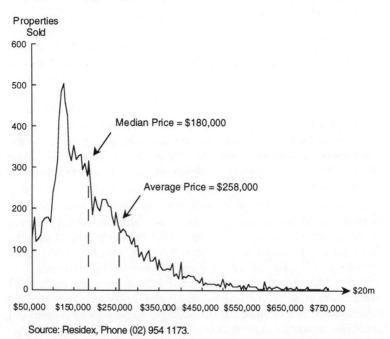

Source: Residex, Phone (02) 954 1173.

You must also understand that although we can generalise about the median price of property in a particular city such as Sydney, median-priced property within the city can vary greatly from suburb to suburb and even from street to street. The table below shows that while the Sydney median price is about $180,000, in a suburb such as Penrith, it is $125,000, but for Woollahra, it is $555,000.

Sydney Median-Priced Residential Property (Selected Suburbs, Dec Qtr, 1993)

Sydney Suburb	Median Price
Bankstown	$167,000
Ku-ring-gai	$383,500
Penrith	$125,000
Sutherland	$235,000
Wollondilly	$118,500
Woollahra	$555,000

Source: Residex and the Real Estate Institute of NSW

Obviously, median prices vary quite significantly, and you should only use it as a guide to selecting the most "reasonable" type of investment property. I must also mention one further point in relation to "median-price". Rental yields on median-priced properties in the more expensive suburbs tend to be low, while at the other end of the scale, median-priced properties in the less expensive areas may be a little more difficult to rent.

Consequently, the term "median-price" should be used only as a guide to selecting a "reasonable" investment property and consideration must be given to both the location and yield. Perhaps it might be easier to think of "reasonable" or "median-price" in a different way. Consider a scale of one to ten where the one-bedroom fibro shack is a "1" and the waterside mansion is a "10", and aim for property in the 3 to 5 category.

So now that you have a better understanding of median-priced property, let's look at why it is such a good vehicle for building wealth. Perhaps its greatest attribute is that it can produce high returns with low risk, making it a very secure investment. The low risk allows it to be highly geared (see page 78 for an explanation of gearing), enhancing the returns even further. And it is this ability to be geared that makes it easily affordable. There is no need for cash deposits and the tax advantages can reduce the weekly costs to less than $100 per week for the average investor buying the average property. Let's look into these in more detail.

High Returns — Low Risk?

Within the financial industry, it is usually believed that higher returns automatically mean higher risks. High returns, the pundits say, usually come with a high risk of losing your capital. Many a worried investor has, then, naturally wondered (as one financial commentator has put it): *Will I get a return of my capital as well as on my capital?*

So it seems a paradox to even suggest that it is possible to achieve high returns with a low risk. But all available evidence shows that it can be the case, by investing in median-priced residential property for the long term. Before we look at this evidence, though, it is essential to understand what I mean by "return" and "risk".

Intuitively we think of a risky investment as one where there is a high likelihood of losing one's capital and so, I will consider "risk" in relation to the potential for the capital base to grow or shrink in size, and "return" in so far as it means the growth in capital relative to inflation. ("Returns" should also take into account the tax refunds, expenses, rents and everything else pertaining to the financial aspects of a property, and I will deal with this in Chapter 10.)

Capital growth rates of median-priced residential property in all capital cities and major towns have been well documented by BIS Shrapnel, the Real Estate Institutes in all States, and by Residex and the Australian Bureau of Statistics. Analysis of the data shows that while median prices may differ in each of the markets, the growth trends are similar. The graph on the opposite page plots the values of median-priced residential property in all capital cities. Melbourne and Sydney data go back as far as 1960.

There are two important points to note in relation to this analysis. First, in all cities the annual capital growth trend has averaged about 11%. More important than the size of the growth, though, is the fact that this growth has outperformed that of shares at 7.0%, and that of inflation at 7.9% over the same time frame. It is *this* growth over and above inflation that has enabled such high returns from property.

Some of you will be wondering what might happen if capital growth did not exceed inflation. The long term data (1900 - 1994) suggests there is a link between capital growth and rental yields, such that when growth is low, yields are high, and vice versa. This scenario was typified in an advertisement that appeared in the Queensland *Courier Mail* of June, 1930 during the depression when capital growth was low, but yields were high.

*Good investment, large residence, on tram and busy trade position, £530, returns £78 yearly, **net return 12 per cent**. Great potential value. John Tritton & Co, 356 Queen St. Phone B6766.*

Median-Priced Residential Property
Time — Not Timing

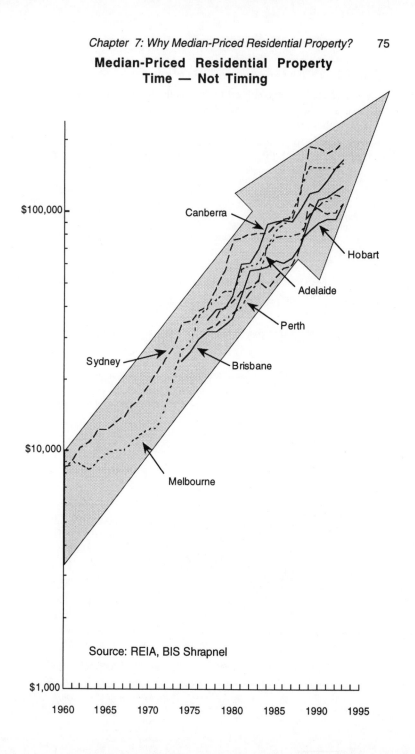

Source: REIA, BIS Shrapnel

But what about the risk involved in achieving capital growth in excess of inflation? This brings us to the second point.

The shape of the graph on the previous page, being relatively free of the extreme highs and lows that characterised the share graph (see page 67), indicates that the growth in value of median-priced residential property is not as volatile as the growth in shares. To the investor, this means that the time over which the property is held is much more important than the timing of the purchase or the timing of the sale. Perhaps we should look more closely at this volatility so that you will understand why there is so little risk involved in investment in median-priced residential property compared to shares.

The graph below was produced by superimposing the annual growth rates for Sydney median-priced residential property on to the share graph shown on page 66. Although I have used Sydney data, any capital city data produces similar results, as is shown by the stable trend patterns in the graph on the previous page.

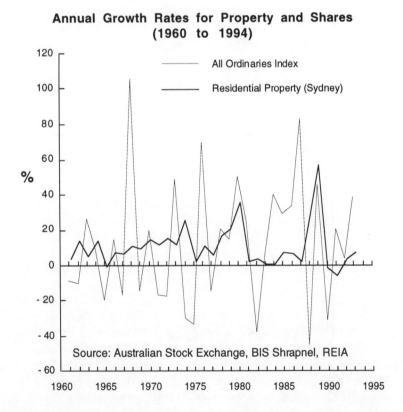

Annual Growth Rates for Property and Shares (1960 to 1994)

All Ordinaries Index

Residential Property (Sydney)

Source: Australian Stock Exchange, BIS Shrapnel, REIA

Let me remind you that a *fall* in growth rates simply indicates a *lower* growth rate, rather than a fall in the capital value and that capital is lost only when the growth rate line crosses the axis and becomes negative.

What do we learn from this graph? First, you *can* make a lot of money by investing in shares. In some cases, the growth in the value of shares has been an astronomical 100% in one year — well above the peaks of property. However, although you can make heaps of money in the share market, it's a small chance, and the risk is that you can also lose heaps of money. In many years, the annual growth rate of shares has been negative, resulting in large capital losses. In some years this loss has exceeded 50%.

Now, what about median-priced residential property? Although it is highly unlikely that you will make a 100% profit in one year, it is also highly unlikely that you will lose any of your capital. Even in the short term, median-priced residential property *rarely* experiences negative growth and it is far less volatile than the share market.

The fact that high returns can be achieved by investing in median-priced residential property with minimal risk has also been confirmed by Residex (1992). Using several different measures of risk, they undertook a most comprehensive study of the risk and return associated with various asset sectors over many different time frames (up to 12 years).

The measures of risk in their analysis included the probability of obtaining a negative return, the standard deviation of return, the probability of a below median return, the probability of a lower quartile return and the probability of a below CPI return. The assets selected were Residential Property (Sydney median prices), Treasury Notes, Commercial Property, Property Trusts, and shares as measured by the All Ordinaries Index. The director of Residex, Dean Dwonczyk, summarised the results like this:

In addition to their good long term returns, the housing market also manages to attain a low risk environment for these returns. For five different definitions of risk, the analysis revealed that residential dwellings, in the long term (five to twelve years), generally attained its above average returns with below average risk.

And here-in lies the key to successful investment in residential property — high returns with low risk *can* be achieved but only by investing for the *longer term* in median-priced residential property. (I should also qualify this statement by suggesting that investment should be in an area with sound growth potential, such as the cities or larger provincial towns.)

Of course the question then arises, how long is long term? Investment in residential property is *not* a "get-rich-quick" scheme. I contend that the property must be held for a minimum of seven years, but preferably for longer, to achieve the high returns available with a minimum of risk.

High Gearing Ability

In a recent advertisement by one of the major banks, the headline read:

Use your home to invest in shares.

I have never once seen an advertisement that reads "Use your shares as collateral to invest in shares." The reason being of course, that very few financial institutions are willing to take a "mortgage" or so called "scrip lien" over shares as a security for buying more shares. If this does happen, the maximum loan to value ratio is usually less than 50%, because the capital value of shares is so unstable. Commercial property and upmarket residential property are treated by the financial institutions with similar caution for exactly the same reasons, and can be borrowed against to a maximum of only about 70%.

On the other hand, median-priced residential property can be borrowed against for as high as 95% of its value because of the high regard banks hold for the stability of its value. The fact that banks are willing to lend so much against its value is further testament to its low risk stature. This mortgaging ability makes median-priced residential property an attractive vehicle for building wealth. "Mortgaging" is a term synonymous with "gearing". But what is gearing and how does it work in your favour?

To gear something, in the technical sense, means to use a small effort to move a large object, thereby gaining a mechanical advantage. On a bicycle, for example, gearing allows the pedals, which have a very small rotation, to turn the large back wheel. Likewise, by using a crowbar, you only need a small effort to lift or lever a large load. The diagram below shows the gearing, or leverage effect of using a crowbar to lift a large load of 600 kg using a small push down effort of just 10 kg.

Crowbar Leverage

A weight of 10 kg plus a crowbar gives you the leverage to move and control a weight of 600 kg.

We can measure the gearing ratio, or leverage, of this crowbar action with the formula:

$$\text{Leverage} \; = \; \frac{\text{Load}}{\text{Effort}}$$

$$= \; \frac{600 \text{ kg}}{10 \text{ kg}}$$

$$= \; 60$$

In this case, the leverage (or mechanical advantage or gearing ratio), is measured by dividing the total weight controlled (600 kg) by the effort needed (10 kg), which is 60.

In a financial sense, gearing of assets (or leverage as it is known in America), has a similar effect. A small amount of money can control a large asset — using the crowbar of the financial industry — a loan. The higher you are geared, the more money you have borrowed and the greater the financial advantage you achieve. Let's see how this works for property.

Gearing or leverage in property is determined in the same way as we measure leverage for crowbars. However, in this case, the load is the size of the asset controlled and the effort applied is the deposit. The formula is:

$$\text{Gearing or Leverage of Property} \; = \; \frac{\text{Asset Value}}{\text{Deposit (Equity)}}$$

Now, applying the formula: Suppose you have $140,000 in cash to invest in property. You could put it all into just one property and borrow nothing. Alternatively, you could put $28,000 into each of five properties with a total value of $700,000 and borrow $112,000 for each (total loan of $560,000). The table below gives you the gearing ratio in each of these situations. As you can see, with no loan and no gearing, the gearing ratio is simply 1, while for a deposit of $140,000 spread over 5 properties, together with a loan of $560,000, the ratio is 5.

Measuring Gearing Ratios in Property

	No Gearing	Gearing
Asset Value	$140,000	$700,000
Deposit (Equity)	$140,000	$140,000
Loan	$0	$560,000
Gearing Ratio	1	5

If you think of the loan of $560,000 as a lever, then the chart below gives you a graphic representation of how a deposit of just $140,000 enables you to control 5 properties with a total value of $700,000.

Loan Leverage

A deposit of $140,000 plus a

loan of $560,000 gives you the

leverage to own and control

5 properties worth $700,000.

How does gearing work in your favour? And what does this mean as regards securing a financial advantage for you? When your property grows in value, gearing can magnify the gain even further. How this happens is illustrated in the table on the next page. Here you see how, for an initial outlay of $140,000, the equity builds much faster when the gearing level is higher. With one property, for example, 10% growth would result in a $14,000 capital gain (10% of $140,000). But with the same growth of 10%, on the same outlay of $140,000, for 5 properties there would be a gain of $70,000 (10% of $700,000 or 5 times $14,000)!

Gearing Effect over Time (10 Yrs)

	No Gearing (1 Property)		Gearing (5 Properties)	
Yr	Property Value	Equity	Property Value	Equity
0	$140,000	$140,000	$700,000	$140,000
1	$154,000	$154,000	$770,000	$210,000
2	$169,400	$169,400	$847,000	$287,000
3	$186,340	$186,340	$931,700	$371,700
4	$204,974	$204,974	$1,024,870	$464,870
5	$225,471	$225,471	$1,127,357	$567,357
6	$248,019	$248,019	$1,240,093	$680,093
7	$272,820	$272,820	$1,364,102	$804,102
8	$300,102	$300,102	$1,500,512	$940,512
9	$330,113	$330,113	$1,650,563	$1,090,563
10	$363,124	$363,124	$1,815,620	$1,255,620

With growth of 10% over 10 years, one property worth $140,000 would have increased in value to $363,124. With no gearing, the equity would be equal to just the property value. However, with 5 properties worth a total of $700,000, and a loan of $560,000, these properties would have increased in value to $1,815,620 — giving an equity of $1,255,620 ($1,815,620 - $560,000)!

Now I'm not suggesting for one minute that you should rush out and buy 5 properties all at once — even if you had the $140,000, you may still have trouble servicing the loan. But the point is that over time, it is possible to accumulate much more wealth through gearing.

But, be warned. Gearing can magnify the returns both forwards and backwards. In other words, losses *as well* as gains can be magnified. *So the secret to successful gearing is to borrow to invest for the long term in a highly stable investment — median-priced residential property in any of the larger cities and towns.* You will not find any 10 year period in our history where such property has ever dropped in value.

For the average person, wealth can only be achieved by gearing. It can make your money work harder and increase your net worth faster than by any other means. So if you've worked through the exercises in Chapter 5, and realised that you need to take drastic action to improve your nest egg, you should now understand how gearing can get you where you want to be much faster. And, if you use median-priced residential investment property as the vehicle, it will get you there with the least risk.

High Affordability

Earlier, I suggested that even average-income earners could easily afford to borrow to buy residential investment property. At less than $100 per week, it costs no more than it does to run the second family car. The fact that low-income earners can and do buy negatively geared property was verified in a report entitled "A Profile of Private Rental Housing Investors" by the Housing Industry of Australia.

The report reveals that 6.5% of negatively geared property investors have *household* incomes of less than $20,000 per year. About 30% have *household* incomes of less than $30,000 per year and more than 40% have *household* incomes of less that $50,000 per year. (It is important to note that these are *household* incomes, and that the income of the individual investor who purchased the property was probably much less.)

Yes, high-income earners do own negatively geared property — but so do many low- and average-income earners. So let's forget about the claims that negatively geared property falls only in the realms of the rich.

But how can low-income earners possibly afford to buy property? There are several reasons, all relating to the fact that residential property can be highly geared. First, a cash deposit may not be needed. Contrary to popular misconceptions, you *don't* need thousands of dollars to get started, but you do need some collateral.

Secondly, because property can be negatively geared, the resulting tax benefits lessen the burden of the loan payments. These tax concessions are second to none, as confirmed by a recent EPAC report ("Income Tax and Asset Choice in Australia" by Howard Pender of the Australian National University and Steven Ross from EPAC), which ranked negatively geared property at the top of its list of tax effective investments. The report said:

From a tax point of view, the least attractive option for an individual with a dollar of savings is to place it in an interest bearing account.... (however) *geared property investment is highly tax favoured.*

Let me demonstrate to you why buying residential investment property is so affordable. To do this, we'll look at the situation of a typical couple, Bill and Mary, purchasing a typical investment property. Suppose that Bill, the principal income earner, earns $45,000 per year and that Mary works part time for $6,000 per year. Let's also suppose that they have already paid off their own home and that they purchase an investment property worth $140,000 in Bill's name only. Let's answer the questions that everyone wants to know. How much will they need to borrow? How will they borrow the money? And most importantly, how much will it really cost them each week?

How much will they need to borrow?

If Bill and Mary have no cash, they will need to borrow the entire cost of the property, plus all the associated purchasing and borrowing costs. These costs are set out in the table below.

Calculating the Loan Size with No Cash Outlay

	Sub Total	Total
Purchase Price		$140,000
Purchasing Costs		
Government Stamp Duty (Qld)	$3,650	
Conveyancing Fees	$350	
Total Purchasing Costs		$4,000
Borrowing Costs		
Establishment Fee	$400	
Mortgage Stamp Duty	$584	
Mortgage Insurance	$146	
Mortgagee's Solicitor's Fees	$420	
Valuation Fees	$150	
Registration on Mortgage	$200	
Miscellaneous Fees	$100	
Total Borrowing Costs		$2,000
TOTAL COSTS		$146,000

In this case, Bill and Mary borrowed just the bare costs. But if they had sufficient collateral and could service the extra loan, they could have borrowed extra for "paint money" or "sleep money". The "paint money" would be to pay to paint the property if they thought it was necessary, in which case the actual cost is not tax deductible, but the interest is.

And the "sleep money"? If you don't have a few thousand dollars lying around to cover the times when Murphy's law applies (those times when the rent is a few days late because the agent has gone on holidays, and the interest payments are due early because it is the shortest month of the year, and your car has just broken down) then borrow it and put it in a special account. It helps you sleep much better knowing that all emergencies can be covered.

How will they borrow the money?

Bill and Mary have now worked out that since they have no cash for a deposit, they would need to borrow the entire amount for the property plus all the associated costs, totalling $146,000. But the property they wish to purchase is worth only $140,000. How can they possibly borrow *more* than the value of the property being purchased?

Most people believe that to buy an investment property, they need the cash to pay for the deposit as well as the purchasing and borrowing costs, and then they need to borrow the rest. This misunderstanding arises because this is the method used for buying a first home. The confusion is also understandable, given that most banks have a policy of lending up to 95% of the value of residential property — not 105%, as would be required.

But it's the *total* loan to value ratio (LV ratio) that makes it possible, and in Bill and Mary's case, they can use their own home to provide the additional collateral needed to boost this ratio. The table below sets out the method for calculating the overall ratio, incorporating the additional security.

No-Deposit Borrowing (Own Home Paid Off)

Total Loan	=	**$146,000**
Value of Properties Mortgaged	=	$140,000 (Own Home) +
		$140,000 (Invest Prop)
Total Value of Property	=	**$280,000**
Loan to value ratio	=	$\dfrac{\$146,000}{\$280,000}$
	=	**52%**

We already know that the total loan needed for the investment property is $146,000. To work out the total value of the property mortgaged, we simply add the value of their own home ($140,000) to the value of the investment property ($140,000), giving us a total of $280,000. Dividing the total loan ($146,000) by the total value of all property mortgaged ($280,000) gives us the total loan to value ratio of 52%.

With such a low LV ratio, the banks would welcome Bill and Mary with open arms — providing they could service their loan.

It would have even been possible for Bill and Mary to have borrowed to buy an investment property *before* they had paid off their own home. To do this, they must be able to service both the existing home loan and the new investment property loan.

The table below shows you how to calculate the LV ratio if there had been an existing home loan of, say, $60,000. The total value of the properties being mortgaged would not have changed. However, the total loan would then include the existing home loan, as well as the investment property loan, bringing the total to $206,000.

No-Deposit Borrowing (Own Home NOT Paid Off)

Loan for Investment Property	=	$146,000	(Price + Costs)
Existing Home Loan	=	$60,000	
Total Loan	=	**$206,000**	
Value of Properties Mortgaged	=	$140,000	(Own Home) +
		$140,000	(Invest Prop)
Total Value of Property	=	**$280,000**	
Loan to value ratio	=	**$206,000**	
		$280,000	
	=	**73.5%**	

In this situation, the LV ratio would be 73.5%, which is still low enough to enable the loan to proceed — but again it would depend on the ability of Bill and Mary to handle the loan payments on both the existing $60,000 loan as well as the new loan of $146,000. However, as we'll see next, *servicing the debt on an investment property is much easier than servicing the debt on your own home*, making it possible to buy an investment property *before* you have fully paid out your own home loan.

If we return to the original situation of Bill and Mary, in which they have paid out their own home loan, the next step is to work out how they are going to pay for the loan as well as the expenses. The mere thought of it is enough to frighten most people away — and it does.

But let's look at the overall picture, so that we can break down the cost of borrowing the $146,000 to buy the investment property to just $47 per week.

How much will the property really cost?

It seems incredible that a $140,000 investment property can cost as little as $47 per week, but step by step I'll show you how to work this out. Let's assume that the loan is an interest-only loan, fixed at 10%. The formula for calculating the real cost of a negatively geared property is:

Real Cost   =   Expenditure   —   Income

          = (Expenses + Loan Payment)   — (Rent + Tax Refund)

Total Expenditure

The expenditure consists of the property expenses, such as agent's fees, rates, insurance, and maintenance, etc., as well as the loan payment. The expenditure for this particular property is set out in the table below.

Total Expenditure on a $140,000 Investment Property

	Sub Total	Total
Property Expenses		$2,340
Loan Payment		
Interest (10% of $146,000)	$14,600	
Principal	0	
Total Loan Payment	$14,600	$14,600
TOTAL EXPENDITURE		$16,940

The total expenditure ($16,940) is the sum of the property expenses ($2,340) and the loan payment ($14,600), which in this case is interest only. (Note that for a principal and interest loan, the loan payment would include both a principal and interest component.)

Total Income

The total income consists of both the rental income and the tax refund and these calculations are shown in the table on the next page. The rental income is $9,360, but working out the tax refund takes a few more steps.

In calculating the tax refund, many people assume that the expenditure is the same as the tax deductions. This is wrong, however, for the two values differ in two very important ways. First, the principal component of a loan payment is an item of expenditure but not a tax deduction. And secondly, the non-cash deductions are tax deductions, but not items of expenditure. Non-cash deductions include the depreciation of the fittings (carpets, stoves, curtains, etc.), the depreciation (or capital allowance) on new buildings and the borrowing costs (written off over five years or less, depending on the term of the loan).

Total Income on a $140,000 Investment Property

	Sub Total	Total
Rental Income	**$9,360**	**$9,360**
Tax Calculation		
Tax on $45,000	$12,582	
New Income ($45,000 + $9,360)	$54,360	
Tax Deductions		
Interest	$14,600	
Property Expenses	$2,340	
Depreciation on Fittings (non cash)	$2,800	
Depreciation on Building (non cash)	$2,000	
Borrowing Costs (non cash)	$400	
Total Deductions	$22,140	
New Taxable Income ($54,360 - $22,140)	$32,220	
Tax on $32,220	**$7,428**	
Tax Refund ($12,582 - $7,428)	**$5,154**	**$5,154**
TOTAL INCOME		**$14,514**

The tax deductions include the interest, property expenses, depreciation on fittings, depreciation on building and borrowing costs, and in this case amount to $22,140, which is substantially more than the cash expenditure of $16,940. On a salary of $45,000, Bill's tax should be $12,582, but his new taxable income of $32,220 ($54,360 - $22,140) attracts tax of only $7,428, creating a tax refund of $5,154. With total rent of $9,360 and a tax refund of $5,154, the total income would be $14,514.

Real Cash Cost

We can now work out the real cost of the property to Bill and Mary. With total expenditure of $16,940 and total income of $14,514, the real cost is just $2,426 per year or $47 per week!

Real Cost = Expenditure - Income
            = $16,940   - $14,514
            = $2,426 per year
            = **$47 per week**

And this is just in the first year! With rental increases over time, the cost per week becomes less until finally the cash flow is positive. Can you see now why borrowing to buy investment property is so affordable?

8
Building Wealth through Investment Property

My friend Jean is a real expert at making fruit cakes. She has followed the same basic recipe for many years, and her cakes are always perfect. But although the basic recipe is still the same, many things have changed with time. Some of the ingredients have altered slightly — the dried fruit is a different brand and is now pre-diced; the eggs now come from the local supermarket instead of from her own backyard hens; and her oven is not the same — she now has a new fan-forced oven instead of an old wood stove.

With each change, Jean baked her fruit cake with a little trepidation, wondering if it would turn out to be the same — only to find that the basic fruit cake recipe still worked, no matter what brand of ingredient she used, no matter where the ingredients came from and no matter what kind of oven she baked her cakes in.

Now you must be wondering what making fruit cakes has got to do with investing in property. In principle, everything. Good recipes just keep on working no matter what. My previous book, *Building Wealth through Investment Property*, was based on a recipe for an early, wealthy retirement that involved borrowing, buying and keeping residential rental property for the long term. The ultimate aim was to retire on the rental income from the properties enabling a financially independent retirement, free of Government handouts.

The recipe I propounded in that book was not new, I certainly didn't invent it, and neither did I have a franchise on it. It is a recipe that had been used successfully by many people for many years *before* we began using it for ourselves more than twenty years ago. The only problem is that this recipe of borrowing to buy and accumulate residential investment properties is *so simple*, that most people overlook it.

But since the early nineties, when my book *Building Wealth through Investment Property* was written, many changes have taken place. There is a growing community awareness of the problems our Governments face in funding future age pensions, with the result that social attitudes to self reliance in retirement are changing. This has occurred simultaneously with a changing investment climate that has brought with it the lowest inflation levels in decades. And so, at a time when people are *thinking* about the possibility of investing for their future, they are also *wondering* if the simple age-old recipe for building wealth through investment property still works in these changing economic times.

Today, I believe that this "old" recipe for retiring early and wealthy is still the best recipe. I believe that this *simple* recipe for building wealth through investment property is just as valid today, as it was yesterday — as it will be tomorrow. And in the next few chapters I will explain why this principle has not, and will not alter, despite the changes to some of the ingredients.

Inflation rates, interest rates, capital growth rates, tax rates, vacancy rates, and most other rates that you could possibly think of have changed in the past few years. However, as you'll see later in Chapters 10 to 12, these changes do not affect the basic recipe of building wealth. In those chapters, I do a detailed analysis of property investment and spell out in very simple language why the basic recipe has not changed.

In this chapter, however, I would like to go through the recipe again, using different figures, so that you can be reassured and see for yourself that the recipe still works today. To do this, we will follow the lives of a typical couple, Bill and Mary, from the time they first leave school. We go through the steps of how they set about saving money as soon as they start work and follow them through the stages of buying their first home, their first investment property, and then look ahead to see how it would be possible for them to build a portfolio of properties. Eventually, we look at how they could retire by the time they reach their mid-forties and live financially independent for the rest of their lives. Although I outlined a similar plan in my previous book, the figures have now been changed to reflect the changing times, but as you'll see, the end result is exactly the same.

Bill and Mary are not real, and the following story never happened. But it could have and it still can, because the recipe they follow is a simple "fruit cake" recipe that *you* can use yourself by varying the ingredients to suit. The recipe for success is outlined on the opposite page. You should read it, copy it, pin it up and read it again and again so that you firmly understand the principle of building wealth through investment property. Then you will be ready to follow Bill and Mary.

Recipe for Success

Step 1: *B*egin With Your First Home

- **Begin with a goal:** Decide when you would like to retire. Work out the assets you will need to give you the income you require for a more than comfortable retirement.

- **Bank your savings:** Start saving as early as possible, so that when you buy your first home, you'll already have a large deposit.

- **Buy your first home:** Borrow to buy your first home (with a P&I loan). Make sure it is within your means. All the mod cons will come later.

- **Build equity in your own home:** Pay off your home loan as fast as possible, although there is no need to completely pay it off before you start the next step.

Step 2: *B*uy an Investment Property

- **Borrow against your equity:** Use your own home as collateral to borrow the entire amount for your first investment property, plus the associated costs. Ideally, the loan should be fixed-rate, interest-only.

- **Buy your first investment property:** As a general guide, look for property around the median-price, in a reasonable location and in a region with long-term sustainable growth (normally a large city or town).

Step 3: *B*uild a Property Portfolio

- **Buy more properties:** As cash flows increase, refinance to buy more and more properties using the growing equity as collateral. Use Section 221D of the Tax Act to enhance cash flows.

- **Be careful:** Be prepared for "Murphy". Budget carefully and learn to handle large sums of money. Set up access to credit lines. Keep some cash on hand. Fix the interest rate for at least three years. Take out insurances. Set reasonable rents. Maintain the property.

- **Be patient:** Stay committed and disciplined as you wait for cash flows and values to increase. Don't fall into the trap of thinking that the grass is greener elsewhere. Don't sell just to see how much you have made.

Step 4: *B*alance the Debt on Retirement

- **Balance the debt:** When you retire, rents become your main source of income. Manipulate the debt levels by selling one or more properties to reduce the loan so that you now have a positive cash flow.

- **Buy Luxuries:** Enjoy your retirement. Buy all the luxuries you want.

Begin with Your First Home

Bill and Mary are average people with no special financial skills. But, from a very early stage in their adult lives, they both had a strong desire to be financially independent by the time they reached 45 years of age.

Bill left school at age 17 and took up a plumbing apprenticeship. He lived at home for the next six years and was able to save more than half his wage, which averaged about $12,000 per year for five years and $25,000 per year when he had finished his apprenticeship. During this time, he saved enough to buy a small car, and also put extra aside in the bank. By the time he was 23, he had saved $25,000, including interest.

Mary was 15 years old when she left school to become an apprentice hairdresser. She averaged just $8,000 per year gross for her first five years before becoming a fully trained hairdresser earning $20,000 per year. Mary lived at home during this time, and by age 23, she had saved $10,000. She didn't buy a car, but in that time, she did save enough for a trip to England.

Bill and Mary married when they were both aged 23. Between them they had managed to save $35,000, which they put towards a house they bought for $100,000. They paid $30,000 as a deposit, used the remaining $5,000 for stamp duty, etc. and some inexpensive furniture, and borrowed $70,000 from a building society. The house, on the outskirts of Brisbane, was a "no frills" three bedroom, 10 square, low-set brick.

Over the next six years, they repaid the $70,000 debt, despite the high interest rates in the early years. To do this, they used 50% of Mary's wages for two years (after which they decided to start a family) and 45% of Bill's wages. The table below shows how they achieved this. In the first year they put $21,000 into the loan, but with high interest rates (interest was $11,000 that year), the principal was reduced to only $60,000. After six years, Bill and Mary owed nothing on a house now worth $140,000.

Paying Off Your First Home in Six Years

End of Year	Bill's Contribution	Mary's Contribution	Principal ($70,000)	Annual Interest
1	$11,000	$10,000	$60,000	$11,000
2	$12,000	$11,000	$46,000	$9,000
3	$13,000	-	$38,000	$5,000
4	$14,000	-	$28,000	$4,000
5	$15,000	-	$15,000	$2,000
6	$16,000	-	0	$1,000

Buy an Investment Property

At 29 years of age, Bill and Mary had paid out the debt on their own home, and were almost ready to embark on the second stage of their plan to be financially independent by age 45. Bill's plumbing business was now clearing $45,000 per year and Mary was now working part-time from home as a hairdresser, earning $6,000 per year.

They now saved the payments they had previously put towards their home loan mortgage so that they could buy a bigger car to accommodate their growing family. These savings, together with Mary's wage, were deposited in a savings account in Mary's name to minimise the tax payable on the interest. After one year, they had saved not only enough for a good second-hand car ($15,000), but also an extra $7,000 for a return trip to England to introduce their two children to their grandparents.

On returning from England, Bill and Mary, now both aged 30, were ready to start investing for their future. They had already looked at their options, and had decided that normal superannuation was not going to be enough. And even if it was, they realised that they would not be able to access their money until they were aged 55, which was far too late because they wanted to reap the rewards of their investing much earlier than that. They were also aware that by investing in shares, they would not only be dealing with a volatile market, but that they would be limited in their capacity to borrow money. Gearing, they had decided, was the only way to build wealth and by borrowing to invest in residential property, they could borrow with very little risk and maximise their returns.

Bill and Mary were very cautious people and having made up their own mind about investment property, decided to talk to others about their ideas. They went to the trouble of finding an accountant who had investment property of his own and who was well versed in the subject. He suggested that they take a fixed-rate, interest-only loan and that the properties be bought in Bill's name in order to maximise the tax benefits. He also told them that as soon as they had bought the properties, they should apply to the Taxation Office for a variation of Bill's PAYE tax, as allowed under Section 221D of the Tax Act.

After finding a real estate agent who understood property investment, and having "done the rounds" of many financial institutions, they decided to buy two properties, each worth $140,000, and took a fixed-rate interest-only loan at 10%. The details of one of the properties and the loan are summarised on the following page. This property will be referred to from now on as the "example property", but I must point out that it is in no way intended that this particular example be representative of an ideal investment property, nor that the loan be an ideal loan.

Example Property

$140,000

Property Description

The example property is a new, three bedroom, low-set brick house with carport, carpets, fencing, etc.

Property Details

Purchasing Costs

Stamp Duty	=	$3,650
Conveyancing Fees	=	$350
Total	=	**$4,000**

Capital Allowance

Construction Cost	=	$80,000
Capital Allowance (2.5%)	=	**$2,000**

Depreciable Items

Value of Fittings	=	$10,300
Tax claim (1st yr)	=	**$2,800**

Property Expenses

Commission (7.5%)	=	$702
Letting Fee	=	$180
Rates	=	$1,000
Insurance	=	$130
Maintenance	=	$228
Other	=	$100
Total (1st yr)	=	**$2,340**

Loan Details

Borrowing Costs

Establishment Fee	=	$400
Mortgage Stamp Duty	=	$584
Mortgage Insurance	=	$146
Bank's Solicitor's Fees	=	$420
Valuation Fees	=	$150
Registration Fees	=	$200
Miscellaneous Fees	=	$100
Total	=	**$2,000**
Tax Claim (1st of 5yrs)	=	$400

Loan Payment Costs

Loan Type	=	Interest Only
Loan Amount	=	$146,000
Interest Rate	=	10%
Loan Payment	=	**$14,600**

Rent Details

Gross Rent (1st yr)	=	**$9,360**
Net Rent (1st yr)	=	**$7,020**

Please note that this example is in no way intended to represent an ideal investment property or an ideal loan. This particular example is the one that has been used throughout this book.

The properties that Bill and Mary bought were both new low-set brick houses complete with carpets, curtains and fencing — in fact everything necessary for a tenant to be able to move into immediately. Bill and Mary took note of all the depreciable items, including the building construction cost, for tax purposes later. They estimated their rent at $9,360 per year and their expenses in the first year at $2,340 — or 25% of the gross rent.

But, after paying for an almost new car and having just returned from a trip to England, Bill and Mary had only a few thousand dollars left in the bank. How did they manage to borrow the entire amount not only for the two properties, but for the purchasing and borrowing costs as well?

How to Borrow the Money

With no cash deposit, Bill and Mary needed to borrow $292,000, made up of the two properties ($280,000), purchasing costs ($8,000 in total), and borrowing costs ($4,000 in total). They could borrow this large sum of money by using the collateral in their own home ($140,000) as well as that of their two investment properties ($280,000). This gave them a loan to value ratio of 69.5% that was worked out as follows:

No-Deposit Borrowing for Two Investment Properties

Loan for 2 properties	=	$140,000	(Invest Prop 1) +
		$6,000	(Costs) +
		$140,000	(Invest Prop 2) +
		$6,000	(Costs) +
Total loan for 2 properties	= **$292,000**		
Value of 3 properties mortgaged	=	$140,000	(Own Home) +
		$140,000	(Invest Prop 1) +
		$140,000	(Invest Prop 2)
Total value of properties mortgaged	= **$420,000**		
Loan to value ratio	= **$292,000**		
	$420,000		
	= **69.5%**		

Bill and Mary had more than enough collateral to borrow to buy the two investment properties, but how were they able to afford the loan? There are two ways of looking at this — from the point of view of the bank, and from the point of view of Bill and Mary.

Bank's Budget

First, the bank had its own set of rules and regulations based on the following formula (which may vary from bank to bank).

$$30\% \text{ of Income} \quad + \quad 80\% \text{ of Rent} \quad \geq \quad \text{All Loan Payments}$$

This means that 30% of their total income (the total of Bill and Mary's wages), plus 80% of the rent (i.e. allowing 20% for rates, insurance, etc.) must be equal to, or greater than their total loan repayments (including their own home loan, if any, other loans, if any, and the two investment property loans). So in the case of Bill (wage of $45,000) and Mary (wage of $6,000), their loan eligibility would be based on:

Bank's Assessment

$$30\% \text{ of } \$51,000 \quad + \quad 80\% \text{ of } \$18,720 \quad \geq \quad 10\% \; \$292,000$$
$$\$15,300 \quad + \quad \$14,976 \quad \geq \quad \$29,200$$
$$\$30,276 \quad\quad \text{which is} \quad \geq \quad \$29,200$$

Hence, Bill and Mary qualified for the loan. Notice how the bank does not take into account the tax refund. Nor do they acknowledge that most, if not all of a second wage can be put to loan payments. Nevertheless, in the eyes of the bank, Bill and Mary would qualify for their loan. Let's see how it looks through the eyes of Bill and Mary.

Bill and Mary's Budget

Bill and Mary had never borrowed so much money before and they wanted to reassure themselves that they could indeed service the $292,000 loan. So they prepared their own budget, rather than rely solely on the bank's assessment. Below is the budget Bill and Mary worked out, based on their income and expenditure.

Total Income

Their total income included both the rental property income and their personal income from their wages. The table below sets out their budget estimates. The total rent was $18,720 ($9,360 from each property). Bill's wage was $45,000 and Mary's wage was $6,000 per year, giving them a total income of $69,720 for the first year.

Personal and Property Income (1st yr)

Property Income	**$18,720**
Personal Income	
Bill's Income	**$45,000**
Mary's Income	**$6,000**
TOTAL INCOME	**$69,720**

Total Expenditure

Bill and Mary's expenditure for the year included the property expenses, loan payments, tax on their wages, and living expenses, and these are set out in the table below.

Total Personal and Property Expenditure (1st yr)

	Sub Total	Total
Property Expenses (25% of Rent)	$4,680	**$4,680**
Loan Payment		
Interest (10% of $292,000)	$29,200	
Principal	0	
Total Loan Payment		**$29,200**
Bill's New Tax Situation (as per 221D)		
New Income ($45,000 + $18,720)	**$63,720**	
Rental Deductions		
Interest	$29,200	
Property Expenses	$4,680	
Depreciation on Fittings (non cash)	$5,600	
Depreciation on Buildings (non cash)	$4,000	
Borrowing Costs (non cash)	$800	
Total Deductions	<u>$44,280</u>	
New Taxable Income ($63,720 - $44,280)	**$19,440**	
Tax on $19,440	**$3,080**	**$3,080**
Mary's Tax		**$0**
Living Expenses		**$16,300**
TOTAL EXPENDITURE		**$53,260**

The first two steps in working out the property expenses and loan payments were relatively easy. Bill and Mary estimated that they would need to allow about 25% of the gross rent for expenses, which totalled $4,680 for the two properties ($2,340 each). And because they had taken an interest-only loan, they knew that their total loan payments would be just the interest component of $29,200 ($14,600 per property, or 10% of $292,000), with no additional payment towards the principal.

Calculating their new tax payable as a result of the negative gearing benefits was a little more involved. This is how they went about it.

Immediately after signing the contracts, Bill and Mary arranged with their accountant to apply for a variation in Bill's tax so that they could have the benefit of the extra money each fortnight, instead of waiting for a tax refund. The 221D application included the following information.

Bill's new income was $63,720, which was the sum of his wages ($45,000) and rents ($18,720). His rental property deductions included the interest ($29,200), expenses ($4,680), depreciation on fittings ($5,600), capital allowance on buildings ($4,000) and borrowing costs ($800). These amounted to $44,280 which he could then offset against his income. As a result, Bill's new taxable income was $19,440 ($63,720 - $44,280), on which he was only required to pay $3,080 in tax, instead of $12,582.

What about Mary's tax? With her income of $6,000 and work-at-home related claims of $600, she paid no tax, because her new income was at the threshold of $5,400. (Had she wanted to, however, she could have earned additional income from Bill by taking care of the financial aspects of his properties. This would allow Bill to get a tax deduction for Mary's fee at a higher marginal rate than she would be paying tax on the extra income.)

Having assessed their new tax situation, Bill and Mary then prepared a personal budget for their day to day living expenses and found that they would need about $16,300 per year for food, clothing and petrol, etc.

Bill and Mary's total personal and property expenditure was $53,260.

Real Cost

The final step for Bill and Mary was to look at the overall picture of their income and expenditure so that they could then gauge for themselves whether they could afford to comfortably buy the properties or not. From the table below, you can see that even with two investment properties, Bill and Mary had an excess of $16,460 ($69,720 - $53,260). In fact, they also worked out that they could have afforded to have bought four properties!

Bill and Mary's Budget in the Beginning

INCOME		EXPENDITURE	
Property income	$18,720	Property expenses	$4,680
		Loan payment	$29,200
Bill's income	$45,000	Bill's new tax	$3,080
Mary's income	$6,000	Mary's tax	$0
		Living expenses	$16,300
TOTAL IN	**$69,720**	**TOTAL OUT**	**$53,260**
EXCESS = Total Income - Total Expenditure = $16,460			

Build a Property Portfolio

Having paid off their first home and taken that gigantic step in buying their first investment property, Bill and Mary, now both aged 30, are well on their way to achieving their goal of financial independence at age 45. But what is the next step for them? Like most people, Bill and Mary would like to know "When can we buy our next property?". Let's look ahead over the next 10 years so that you can see how it might be possible for them to build a property portfolio from a base of their initial two rental properties, and create a net worth of more than one million dollars.

Over time, as wages and rents rise, and property values grow, they will be able to borrow more money, to buy more property to build more net worth. Let's construct a table with all the relevant financial information about Bill and Mary (such as wages, rents, taxes, property values, living expenses, etc.) and project these values over the next 10 years so that you can see how they could do it. But what rates of growth should we use?

In my previous book *Building Wealth through Investment Property,* I produced a table to show people how it was possible to acquire property over time, using growth rates depicting the thirty-year averages at that time. At this point in time, despite the low inflationary regime, these thirty-year averages have not significantly changed. However, many people now want to know if the recipe still works in these changing times.

As a result, in describing a strategy that Bill and Mary might use, I have altered the figures to show you that despite changing times, it is still possible to build wealth through investment property. I have chosen a set of mid-range growth rates based on a combination of data from the 1960s when inflation was low; the Government's projections for the SGC (the assumptions were salary growth of 5.5% and capital growth of 8%), and current levels. These rates are shown in the table below, together with the rates used in my previous book. (However, as I'll show you in Chapter 10, it wouldn't matter what rates we used.)

Yearly Rates of Increase in Spreadsheet Projections

	Building Wealth through Investment Property	*Building Wealth in Changing Times*
Wages	9.5%	6.0%
Rents	8.0%	5.0%
Living Expenses	8.0%	5.0%
Property Values	11.0%	7.5%

Cash Flow is the Key to Buying More Property

Using values of 5% inflation on rents and living expenses, 6% growth on wages and 7.5% property growth, I produced the spreadsheet on the opposite page. How would Bill and Mary know when they could afford to buy their next investment property? The key is not how much equity they have, nor how much they are worth — *cash flow is the key* — and the main factors affecting cash flow are wages, taxes, rents, interest rates, property expenses and living expenses.

Consequently, for Bill and Mary the key indicator is the "excess" cash flow, which is listed in the table at position number 8. This is the money they would have left over if they prepared a budget as they did on page 98. In the beginning, this "excess" was $16,460. After one year, this "excess" would increase due to rising rents and wages, and they could then afford to buy two more properties, each costing $150,500. Their net worth would then have increased to $146,600.

If Bill and Mary prepared a budget each year, they would find that for the next two years they must be patient and wait for their cash flow to increase to the point where they could afford to buy another property. In the third year, if they did their sums for five investment properties, their new budget would be as shown below. The figures have been taken from Year 3 in the table on the opposite page. Bill's wage would have increased to $53,596 and Mary's wage to $7,146 giving a total income of $60,742. The gross rental income from five properties would be $54,177, giving them a total income of $114,919. If their expenditure totalled $114,809, they would then have an excess of $110.

Bill and Mary's Budget for the Third Year

INCOME		EXPENDITURE	
Property income	$54,177	Property expenses	$13,544
		Loan payment	$78,728
		Living expenses	$18,869
Bill's income	$53,596	Bill's new tax	$3,668
Mary's income	$7,146	Mary's tax	$0
TOTAL IN	**$114,919**	**TOTAL OUT**	**$114,809**
EXCESS = Total Income − Total Expenditure = $110			

If Bill and Mary continued this process of budgeting, borrowing and buying properties, after just 10 years they would have seven investment properties, giving them a net worth of more than one million dollars!

Building Wealth through Investment Property

Year	0	1	2	3	4	5	6	7	8	9	10
1 Joint Income	51,000	54,060	57,304	60,742	64,386	68,250	72,344	76,685	81,286	86,163	91,333
2 Tax	12,582	13,337	14,137	14,985	15,884	16,838	17,848	18,919	20,054	21,257	22,532
Tax Refund	9,502	10,072	10,676	11,317	11,996	12,716	13,479	14,287	15,145	16,053	17,017
Tax Payable	3,080	3,265	3,461	3,668	3,888	4,122	4,369	4,631	4,909	5,204	5,516
3 Rent per Property	9,360	9,828	10,319	10,835	11,377	11,946	12,543	13,170	13,829	14,520	15,246
Gross Rent	18,720	39,312	41,278	54,177	56,886	59,730	75,260	79,023	82,974	101,643	106,725
Property Exp.	4,680	9,828	10,319	13,544	14,221	14,932	18,815	19,756	20,743	25,411	26,681
4 Total Income	69,720	93,372	98,581	114,919	121,272	127,979	147,604	155,708	164,260	187,806	198,058
5 Interest	29,200	60,590	60,590	78,728	78,728	78,728	101,260	101,260	101,260	129,251	129,251
6 Living Expenses	16,300	17,115	17,971	18,869	19,813	20,803	21,844	22,936	24,083	25,287	26,551
7 Total Expenditure	53,260	90,798	92,341	114,809	116,650	118,585	146,287	148,582	150,995	185,152	188,000
8 Excess	16,460	2,574	6,240	110	4,622	9,394	1,317	7,126	13,265	2,654	10,059
9 Amount Invested	5,658	21,034	18,955	26,778	24,067	21,214	31,336	27,705	23,885	36,966	32,191
10 Property Value	140,000	150,500	161,788	173,922	186,966	200,988	216,062	232,267	249,687	268,413	288,544
Total Property	420,000	752,500	808,938	1,043,529	1,121,794	1,205,929	1,512,435	1,625,868	1,747,808	2,147,307	2,308,355
Inv Properties	2	4	4	5	5	5	6	6	6	7	7
11 Loans	292,000	605,900	605,900	787,275	787,275	787,275	1,012,597	1,012,597	1,012,597	1,292,514	1,292,514
12 Net worth	128,000	146,600	203,038	256,254	334,519	418,653	499,838	613,271	735,211	854,793	1,015,841
Net worth-Home	-12,000	-3,900	41,250	82,333	147,553	217,665	283,776	381,004	485,524	586,380	727,297

Notes on Building Wealth Table

The strategy depicted for Bill and Mary is in no way intended to be a rigid blue print for others to follow, but rather a recipe that can be altered to suit your own needs. Your situation will no doubt be quite different with factors such as wages, rents, taxes, property values, and both property and personal expenses varying significantly.

Also, the rates at which these values increase may vary depending on capital growth and inflation, and these rates may not increase on a uniform basis. For simplicity, the spreadsheet constructed depicts regular annual rates of increase, but it is more likely that the increases will be "ad hoc" with values such as rents stagnating in some years and increasing by more than the average in other years. This may mean that, although you should be able to afford to buy another property every few years, you may buy none in five years, or four in one year.

So your pathway to wealth may be slower or faster. What is more important is that the principle of building wealth by borrowing to buy and keep residential investment property for the long term, is the same no matter what the conditions.

1. Joint income

Bill and Mary's initial joint income was $51,000 per year and rose by 6% per year. It consisted of Bill's income of $45,000 and Mary's income of $6,000. A lower income simply means that it may take a little longer to build a portfolio. A higher income may accelerate the process. But as we'll see later (see item number 6. Living expenses), the level of income is no more important than how you spend it.

2. Tax

To simplify Bill and Mary's tax situation, tax was calculated at a flat rate of approximately 25% of the combined wage and it was also assumed that about 75% of this tax was refunded. In reality, the tax refund would not be a constant percentage, but would vary from year to year. Also, as allowed under Section 221D of the Tax Act, the tax benefits were accounted for in the year in which they were accrued, not the following year, which would normally be the case with a tax refund.

Furthermore, the tax would depend not only on the total income, but how the income was split between the family members. For example, the total tax for two people on $20,000 and $25,000 would be less than the tax on a single income of $45,000. This is very important with respect to the name(s) in which the property is registered. Property bought in joint names means that both the income and deductions are split, but this may be of no advantage if the spouse is not working.

3. Rent per property

Initial rent was $180 per week ($9,360 per year) and gross rent was the number of properties times the rent. In your case, the rent level would depend on the property, the location and the market. Also, net yields may vary significantly from the 5% net yield I have used. In Bill and Mary's situation, the rental property expenses such as rates, insurances, agent's fees and maintenance, etc., were 25% of the gross rent but in practice, this would vary. Both rents and expenses were increased at 5% per year. However, in other situations, increases may be irregular. Since this affects the cash flows, it may also determine the frequency of acquiring additional properties (more so than the rate of increase in the property value).

4. Total income

Bill and Mary's total income was the sum of their salaried incomes and the gross rent from all of their investment properties. In the first year, this was $69,720.

5. Interest

Bill and Mary took interest-only loans and the rate was assumed to be fixed at 10% for the 10 years. It's more than likely you would encounter a variety of interest rates throughout the process, which would affect the rate of further property purchases. And although I have used an interest-only loan in the example, you may prefer a principal and interest loan. Over a term of 25 years or more, the payment is not significantly extra. Alternatively, you could obtain an interest-only loan but use any excess cash to reduce the debt at each refinance, thereby giving you the equivalent of a "fixed-rate P & I loan" with you retaining control of the principal repayments.

6. Living expenses

Bill and Mary's personal living expenses were initially $16,300 per year and were increased at 5.0% per year. These expenses included their day to day living costs such as food, clothes, car, electricity and holidays, etc. This is perhaps one of the biggest factors that will determine just how quickly you build your wealth. For Bill and Mary, the initial figure of $16,300 was based on Government figures for a typical family of two adults and two children. This does not mean that they would be limited to this amount, for they could well use the excess cash to boost their living expenses, allowing them to have a holiday, to buy another car, or to just spend it on daily extras. Bill and Mary would certainly not be condemned to a life of penance for the time that they would be acquiring properties. And neither would you be. However, you should remember this. A few years of frugality will ensure many years of prosperity.

He is richest whose pleasures are cheapest.

7. Total expenditure

Their total expenditure was the sum of the tax payable, the rental property expenses, the interest on the loan (or both principal and interest payments with a principal and interest loan) and their personal living expenses. In the first year, total expenditure was $53,260.

8. The excess

The excess was the total income less the total expenditure. This was the *key* that would enable Bill and Mary to determine when they could afford to buy their next property. With natural increases in rent and salary, this excess would gradually increase to the point where it would be possible for them to service the loan on yet another property.

In your case, you could use the "excess" for buying luxuries. Or you could put it towards reducing the debt each time you refinance. Or you could save it in a bank account to use as a cash reserve, in which case it would best be put in the name of the lowest income earner to minimise the tax. You could even use some of it as a deposit for another property.

9. Amount invested

The amount invested was the interest less net rent and tax credit. This is the after-tax cash flow, or the actual contribution to the properties.

10. Property value

Bill and Mary's own home and their first two investment properties were each worth $140,000 but they could well have bought one dearer or three cheaper rental properties. The property value increased each year at 7.5% and the total property value included their own home.

In your situation, the property value could vary greatly, as could the style of property. It's important to note that the rate of capital growth does not determine the rate of purchase of more properties. Even if property values doubled overnight, you would be able to buy more property only if your cash flow allowed it.

11. Loans

Loans were the total of the existing loans plus the new loans. All loans included the borrowing and purchasing costs, so each property was bought with a loan amounting to 104.3% of the property value.

12. Net worth

Bill and Mary's net worth could be calculated by either including their own home or not. By the 10th year, Bill and Mary would own a total of eight properties — their own plus seven rental properties. At this stage, their net worth, including their principal residence, would have surpassed one million dollars.

Balance the Debt on Retirement

In showing you how Bill and Mary could possibly build an investment property portfolio, I hope that I have helped answer everyone's question — "When can we buy our next property?" The next most logical question would be — "When can we retire?" Bill and Mary had originally set out to be financially independent by the time they were both 45. Let's look at their position after just 10 years (they would then be aged 40) to see how much further they would need to go to achieve their goal.

Taking the actual figures from the table on page 101, after 10 years, Bill and Mary would have accumulated 7 investment properties, each worth $288,544. But of course they would still have loans of $1,292,514. If they sold 4 investment properties with a total value of $1,154,176 to help reduce the debt, they would be left with 3, and a small debt of $138,338 ($1,292,514 less $1,154,176). If Bill and Mary had saved the excess cash, they could easily eliminate this debt. But let's suppose they spent some of it along the way and that they could reduce the debt to only $50,000.

Let's look at their retirement income in terms of the rent received and interest payable in *today's dollars* (see the table below).

After 10 years, retire completely

Loan size	=	$1,292,514
Total value of 4 properties sold	=	$1,154,176 (4 x $288,544)
Debt left after sale of 4 properties	=	$138,338
Debt left after cash reduction	=	$50,000
Income in today's dollars		
Income from 3 properties	=	$21,000 (3 x $7,000)
Interest owed on remaining debt	=	$3,000
Net income per year	=	$18,000

(This exercise does not take into account CGT, as I am simply assessing a potential income situation. On page 112, ways in which this tax can be minimised are discussed.)

Each of the 3 properties would produce $7,000 net rent (5% net yield on $140,000), giving them a total rental income of $21,000. The interest on the remaining debt of $50,000 ($30,000 in today's dollars), would be $3,000 (in today's dollars). If they were to retire at this stage (at age 40), Bill and Mary would have an indexed income of $18,000 per year, which is greater than most other couples achieve by age 65! (Remember that the average retired couple aged over 65 receives just $15,000 per year!)

Bill and Mary would be well on their way to achieving total financial independence by age 45. But why retire at 40? It's certainly nice to be financially independent at 40, but perhaps Bill and Mary are like many other couples who want to continue to work, even if only on a part-time basis. Let's look at some of their other options.

Retirement Options

After 10 years, retire to part-time work

Suppose Bill and Mary decide to retire from full-time work after 10 years, but continue to work part time for just two days per week each. Their situation might then be:

Income in today's dollars

Net income from 3 properties less interest	=	$18,000
Bill's income (working 2 days per week)	=	$10,000
Mary's income (working 2 days per week)	=	$6,000
Total income		= **$34,000**

After 15 years, retire completely

Bill and Mary's initial goal was to become financially independent by the time they reached 45 years of age. If they had followed their plan for 15 years, they would have accumulated 9 properties and would only need to sell 4 to clear the remaining debt, leaving them with 5 rental properties. Their situation would then be:

Income in today's dollars

Total income from 5 properties	= **$35,000** ($7,000 x 5)

After 20 years, retire completely

If Bill and Mary had continued to work for 20 years, they would have accumulated 12 properties and would need to sell 5, leaving them with 7 properties, no debt, and some cash in hand from the sale. Their situation would then be:

Income in today's dollars

Total income from 7 Properties	= **$49,000** ($7,000 x 7)

There are many other options that Bill and Mary could consider. But as you can see, no matter what they decide, they could be retiring in less than 20 years with a retirement income that few people ever achieve even after a lifetime of work. But what else could Bill and Mary have done?

What else could Bill and Mary have done?

Let's suppose that Bill and Mary invested the money they might have put into property over the years and instead, invested it in either a normal superannuation fund, or in a bank as a term deposit. The amounts invested are shown at position 9 in the table on page 101, except that the time has now been extended to 25 years. We should also look at Bill and Mary's situation had they done nothing but rely solely on a 10% contribution to the SGC. The table below shows the size of the asset accrued in each of the investments over a particular time frame, and to get a true comparison, these values have been converted into *today's dollars*.

After 10 years of investing in property, Bill and Mary would have an equity or net worth of $727,297, as shown in the table on page 101. If we convert this to today's dollars, this would be the equivalent of $446,497. This is almost double that of super ($223,883), three times that of cash ($173,333) and about nine times that accrued in the SGC ($49,169) — and let me keep reminding you — that's if the SGC survives. These figures, along with those for 15, 20 and 25 years, are shown in the table below.

I have always said that property investment is a long-term investment, but is 10 or 15 years really a long time when you consider just how much you can achieve compared to other investments? It should now be obvious that investing in property will allow you to retire sooner and wealthier.

Wealth Accrued in Various Investments (In 1994 Dollars)

	10 yrs	15 yrs	20 yrs	25 yrs
Property	$446,497	$796,533	$1,258,085	$1,813,589
Superannuation	$223,883	$353,407	$510,052	$685,744
Cash	$173,333	$254,344	$344,368	$434,780
SGC	$49,169	$78,446	$111,255	$147,935

Assumptions:

Residential Property: Details as per table on page 101 and extended over 25 years.

Superannuation: Contributions as per property; 2% real rate of return (above inflation); no administrative charges; tax of 15% on contributions; 12% tax on earnings (assuming tax concessions reduce the rate from 15%); 40% tax saving on first $3,000 contribution and 75% of remainder; all tax savings reinvested; no tax on lump sums.

Cash: Contributions as per property; interest at 6%; interest taxed at 40% marginal rate.

SGC: Contributions at 10% of gross income; 2% real rate of return (above inflation); no administrative charges; tax of 15% on contributions; 12% tax on earnings (assuming tax concessions reduce the rate from 15%); no tax on lump sums.

9
Retirement Ready Reckoner

Now that you have seen how a typical couple such as Bill and Mary can build a property investment portfolio that would give them the option to retire early and wealthy, let's get back to your own situation.

Are you ready today to buy your first investment property? Perhaps you are well on the road to wealth and own several investment properties. Maybe you still have a mortgage on your own home and are wondering if you should wait a few more years before buying your next property. It's also possible that you have not bought any property at all and are thinking about buying an investment property as your first home. Or it could be that you have recently left school and have just started your first job.

No matter what your stage of life, you should be setting some goals for your future financial independence. I would like to think that, having read this far, you are now considering residential investment property as your form of super. But how many properties are you going to need to support you in retirement?

In Chapter 5, we went step by step through the process of working out your own retirement scenario. If you go back to pages 54 to 56, you will see just how much income you thought you would need in your retirement and the size of the nest egg needed to produce that income. I suggested that you would need to multiply your desired retirement income by 1.2 to allow for tax, and then by 20, assuming that the asset base produced a 5% yield, after allowing for capital growth. On average, the net (net of expenses), before-tax yield from residential investment properties is about 5%, and the growth more than compensates for inflation.

Now that you understand how it is possible to retire on the rent from a portfolio of investment properties, we need only convert your retirement nest egg into the number of investment properties you would need to own (free of debt) to produce the income you desire in retirement.

How Many Properties will You Need in Your Retirement?

To make it easier to relate to the following calculations, I will convert everything into today's dollars.

Now suppose that you would like to retire in 15 years with an after-tax income of $25,000. Allowing for tax, this would be the equivalent of about $30,000 before tax. For a net yield of 5%, you would need to have total assets over and above your own home of $600,000, which would produce a before-tax income of $30,000 (5% of $600,000).

If, after 15 years, you owned median-priced investment property with a total value of $600,000, then one possible scenario would be that you own 5 properties outright, each valued at $120,000 (5 times $120,000). The table below sets out this complete calculation.

Estimating the Number of Properties Needed in Retirement

Income desired (today's dollars, after tax)	= $25,000
Income desired (today's dollars, before tax)	= $25,000 x 1.2
	= $30,000
Nest egg required (today's dollars)	= $30,000 x 20
	= $600,000
Value of 1 property (today's dollars)	= $120,000
Number of Properties Needed	= $\dfrac{\$600,000}{\$120,000}$
	= 5

To own 5 median-priced investment properties outright it might be necessary to accumulate 9 properties, so that when you sell 4 of them to balance the debt on retirement, you would be left with 5 unencumbered. Obviously, if the properties you owned were valued at only $100,000 each, you would need to own 6 properties outright. Or if the properties were valued at $200,000 each, then you would need to own 3, and so on.

In reality, your properties would have a range of values. However, this is purely a guide to get you thinking about the *number* of properties you would need to aim for in retirement. It could also be that you want a much higher income and are prepared to invest for a little longer; it could be that the properties are all of different values; it could be that the rental yield is higher or lower than 5%; it could be that any number of things will differ.

Retirement Ready Reckoner

At least, by now, you should be setting a goal as to the number of properties you would need in your own retirement to provide the income you require, and laying out a plan as to how you are going to achieve it. Filling in this table should be the *final* step in *planning* your retirement.

Retirement Ready Reckoner

Income desired (today's dollars, after tax) = $_____

Income desired (today's dollars, before tax) = $_____ x 1.2

= $_____

Nest egg required (today's dollars) = Income (before tax) x 20

= $_____

Value of 1 property (today's dollars) = $_____

Number of Properties Needed = $\dfrac{\text{Nest Egg Required}}{\text{Value of 1 Property}}$

= _____

If you would like to retire sooner and wealthier than most Australians, the *final* step in planning should be followed by the *first* step in *doing* something about it. This is the "Anti-Lemming Principle".

One further point must be considered in relation to balancing the debt on retirement — the Capital Gains Tax.

Minimising the CGT

Once you are in a position to retire, selling some of the properties to balance the debt will no doubt incur Capital Gains Tax (CGT). And if you sell all the properties while you are still working, this tax could be quite considerable. But although the CGT is a real cost, its effect is cushioned, because tax is paid only on the gains over and above inflation. Also, if we analyse the returns from the properties sold, taking into account the CGT, the after-tax, after-selling costs, after-CGT rate of return is only marginally reduced from about 36% to 30% compound per annum.

Moreover, despite the minimal impact of the CGT, it can be reduced. Below are just a few of the ways in which you can wind down towards retirement and pay a minimum in CGT.

Options to Minimise the CGT

Do Not Sell Any Properties

• Rather than continue to build the portfolio, you could allow the rental income to gradually overtake the interest. This would create a positive cash flow without the need to sell — though at the same time, your tax refund would gradually diminish because of the reduced tax loss.

• Alternatively, if you have some other cash savings at the time of your retirement, perhaps as the result of a superannuation payout, you could use this lump sum to reduce or pay off the debt.

• Or, if you have a lump sum, rather than pay off the debt, its earnings could be used to supplement income and help pay the interest bill, while waiting for rents to increase.

• You could also gradually reduce the debt in the years prior to retirement by either taking a principal and interest loan, or by keeping an interest only loan and making loan reduction payments at each refinance.

Sell Some Properties

• The properties could be sold when your income is lowest, such as when you retire completely from the workforce or when you refinance a large loan and pay the interest up front.

• You could sell the extra properties in a staggered manner instead of all at once. This would then spread the CGT over a number of years, and keep the taxable capital gain within the lower marginal tax rates.

• Or you could sell the properties that attract the least CGT — such as those in the name of the spouse with the lower income, or they could be those properties that have incurred the lowest capital growth relative to inflation.

PART III

Analysing
the Changes

10
Changing Economic Times

The pain of the recession in the early 1990s brought with it major economic changes in Australia. Following the free-spending binge of the late 1980s, the recession "we had to have" produced the 90s hangover of company crashes and long dole queues. According to our political masters and their advisors, the key gain from all the pain of the recession was a new era of low inflation. According to the experts:

Lower inflation will improve the functioning of the price system, reduce remaining distortions in the tax system, enhance the quality of information available for business decisions, and support a more equitable income distribution. It will mean lower interest rates, better saving and investment decisions, less uncertainty and greater efficiency generally.

(1992 EPAC report entitled "Improving Australia's Inflation Performance")

Since early 1990, we have witnessed a dramatic lowering of inflation rates compared to the late 1980s. However, while politicians hail low inflation as an economic saviour, not everyone has the view that it is the best thing since sliced bread. One such group is the retirees who were receiving significant incomes from high interest on bank deposits in the late 80s and who have seen their incomes halved. Is this what the EPAC report meant by a "more equitable income distribution"?

Another group who are uncertain about the impact of economic change are those property investors who believe that high inflation, and therefore high capital growth, are the "be all" and "end all" of property investment. Their already shaky confidence would not have been helped by the financial commentators who saw the lower inflation rates of the 90s as an obituary for property investors. Headlines began appearing along the lines:

Low inflation removes much of the cream from property investing.

and:

Negative gearing is dead!

Influenced by the massive hikes in property values, particularly during the latter half of the 1980s, these commentators created their own fuzzy logic about the relationship between inflation, capital growth and property investment. It was based on the following assumptions.

The Fuzzy Logic of how Inflation affects Capital Growth

High Inflation

    = High Capital Growth

        = Good times for property investment

And conversely:

Low Inflation

    = Low Capital Growth

        = Bad times for property investment

This fuzzy logic was carried over to negative gearing, only this time the theory had a different set of assumptions.

The Fuzzy Logic of how Inflation affects Negative Gearing

High Interest Rates

    = High Tax Deductions

        = High Tax Refund

            = Negative gearing is worthwhile

And conversely:

Low Interest Rates

    = Low Tax Deductions

        = Low Tax Refund

            = Negative gearing is dead

Although the commentators were certainly correct in concluding that lower inflation would undoubtedly lead to lower capital growth and lower tax refunds, a more thorough analysis shows that low inflation does NOT kill property as an investment, and that negative gearing is NOT dead. In fact, as I will show, the long-term returns from investment property are excellent over the entire range of inflation rates that Australia has experienced. What is more startling is that the *real* returns (i.e. after inflation) can be even greater during periods of low inflation.

But first, you need to know how to analyse investment property so that we can make some meaningful comparisons of how changing economic times might affect the returns on investment property.

Understanding the Changes

It would be a mistake to compare the *growth* in value of a property in one situation to that of a property in another, without first knowing what each one has cost along the way. No matter what the investment, or what the situation, in *all* cases you *must* compare the "ins" and "outs".

For most negatively geared rental property, there will be a short-fall between the rent and the combined loan payments and rental expenses, even after the tax refunds are taken into consideration. The series of regular payments that you would need to make to cover this shortfall is referred to as your *after-tax cash flow* and represents the "ins" for the investment. (Note: Any initial deposit would be the first item in the cash flow.)

What you get "out" of a negatively geared property is the equity that you build up over time. At any point, it can be calculated simply as the value of the property less the amount still owing on the loan. You do not need to sell the property to measure how much you have made; you only need to estimate the value of the property. (Note that with time, the rents should gradually overtake the loan payments and property expenses, and then your "outs" will also include this surplus.)

To calculate the return on the investment, we must relate the "outs" to the "ins" for the property (i.e. relating the equity at the end of a set period, say five years, to the after-tax cash flows each year along the way). For the same reason that we compare interest rates from banks as a guide to the best return on cash investments, we work out the "interest rate" you would need to get on your cash flows to get the equity you now have. In this case, the "interest rate" is called the Internal Rate of Return or IRR, and must be calculated by trial and error, taking into account the timing of all the "ins" and "outs".

To more easily understand the analysis, let's go through an example over five years using the example property described on page 94. This $140,000 property was bought by an investor earning $45,000 per year with an interest-only loan of $146,000 (including costs of $6,000). The interest in each of the five years (at 10%) would then be $14,600.

Suppose that in the first year the property rents for $9,360 (i.e. $180 per week), with expenses of $2,340, and that these both increase at 5% per year over the five years. After one year, the investor would be eligible for a tax refund of $5,154. However, in calculating the cash flow, I have assumed that the investor has applied under Section 221D of the Tax Act, to have the refund in the form of a reduction in his PAYE tax. After five years, with annual capital growth of 7.5%, the property would have increased in value to $200,988. Let's look at the "ins" and "outs".

What You Put "In" Over 5 Years

The shortfall in the first year would be $2,426 (rent of $9,360 plus a tax refund of $5,154, less interest of $14,600 and expenses of $2,340). Over five years, the interest is constant (interest-only loan), but both rents and expenses increase with inflation (5%), while the tax refunds decline. The negative after-tax cash flows, which are the "ins", would then be:

The "Ins" over 5 years

	Yr 1	Yr 2	Yr 3	Yr 4	Yr 5
After-tax cash flows	-$2,426	-$2,324	-$2,124	-$1,768	-$1,688

What You Get "Out" at the End of 5 years

For an interest-only loan, the debt is constant over the five year period. Consequently the equity, or what you get "out" after 5 years would be $54,988, which is the difference between the property value after five years (with capital growth at 7.5%) and the loan. It is calculated as follows:

The "Outs" over 5 years

	At Purchase	After 5 Years
Property Value	$140,000	$200,988
Loan	$146,000	$146,000
Equity	-$6,000	$54,988

Relating the "Outs" to the "Ins"

Having worked out the "ins" and "outs", we must now calculate the rate of interest needed to turn all of the "ins" (after-tax cash flows) into the "outs" (equity). In other words, you put in $2,426 in the first year, and "interest" is added. You add $2,324 in the second year and again "interest" is added and so on until you know what "interest rate" was needed to reach the equity. This "rate of interest" is called the Internal Rate of Return or IRR. If you have a few days to spare, the IRR can be worked out by hand using a trial and error method. I prefer to use a computer, which can do it for me in a few milliseconds. (For those without days to spare and who have access to a personal computer, details of the appropriate computer programs are on page 191.)

In this example over five years, the IRR would be 67.57% per year compound. Over 10 years, the IRR would be 36.45% per year compound (time lowers the gearing and tax benefits and hence the return).

Link between Inflation, Capital Growth, and Interest Rates

Now that we have established how to measure investment returns using *all* the relevant factors, it is now possible to analyse the performance of investment property under different inflationary regimes using the IRR. But what inflation rates should we use? Should we look at today's rate of inflation, or yesterday's or tomorrow's?

Furthermore, because inflation, capital growth and interest rates are interdependent, what corresponding values should we use for these other variables? What is their relationship with each other? Is it possible to have low inflation yet high capital growth? Is it possible to have high interest rates with low inflation? Or what about high capital growth coupled with low interest rates?

We know that the trends over the past thirty or so years (1960 to 1994) for each variable were inflation at 8%, capital growth at 11.5% and interest rates at 12%. But to gain an insight into what relationship would allow us to give a realistic appraisal of investment property, let's look at the past few decades, as they have provided a wide range of economic conditions.

Property in the 60s, 70s, and 80s

What exactly did happen to investment property over the past three decades? Everyone remembers the boom times for capital growth of property in the latter half of the eighties. Some may not be old enough to remember the rampant inflation of the Whitlam era of the early seventies. Even fewer will remember the sixties (who remembers the Beatles?), and the lowest inflation of all three decades. Let's take a closer look at capital growth, inflation and interest rates over those decades to see how they related to each other.

The relevant information on the three variables was obtained from the Reserve Bank (interest rates), Australian Bureau of Statistics (CPI), and BIS Shrapnel and the REIA (capital growth of median-priced residential property in Brisbane, Sydney and Melbourne).

Comparing the Past Three Decades

Annual Averages	1960s	1970s	1980s
Inflation (CPI)	3.0%	11.0%	8.0%
Capital Growth	6.5%	14.5%	11.5%
Interest Rate	4.5%	7.5%	13.5%

Source: Reserve Bank, ABS, BIS Shrapnel, and REIA

In the 1960s, average annual inflation for the decade was less than 3%, while capital growth averaged 6.5%. Interest rates averaged somewhere between the two at 4.5%. The 70s saw much higher inflation (11%), but again, it was exceeded by capital growth at 14.5%. Ironically, interest rates did not keep pace with inflation and were a comparatively low 7.5%. The 60s and 70s produced a unique opportunity for property investors. Did you realise that in those decades, you could borrow OPM (Other People's Money) at an interest rate lower than the capital growth rate, put it into property and literally make money out of thin air? In those days, you didn't even have to rent the property to make money. In such cases, the rate of return (IRR) can be so high as to go off the scale! What was the catch? In the 60s and 70s, money was not freely available and it was difficult to borrow money. If you could, the sky was the limit.

However, by the 1980s the story was very different. Capital growth (11.5%) still exceeded inflation (8%), but interest rates (13.5%) were now much higher than either inflation or capital growth. But why the disparity in interest rates between the decades?

Following the deregulation of the financial markets in 1983, money became more freely available — but at a cost of higher real interest rates (relative to inflation). This meant that although it was easy to borrow money, you could no longer make money out of thin air by investing in property. However, despite the relatively high interest rates, the returns, as measured by the IRR, were still very high, though not as high as the returns in the 60s and 70s.

For the many investors and commentators who witnessed the high growth of the 80s, the idea that property investment at that time was not as good as the 60s or 70s may come as somewhat of a shock. If nothing else, it should emphasise the point that high capital growth alone does not necessarily indicate a good investment.

Looking back over the past three decades, there were some obvious similarities but also some glaring differences. The common thread was the fact that capital growth consistently exceeded inflation by several per cent. This difference can be attributed to factors other than inflation that also cause property to increase in value, namely scarcity and improvements (such as rezoning or renovations). However, the major difference between the decades was the interest rates which, in real terms, were exceedingly high in the 80s compared to either the 60s or 70s.

So what can we learn from the past? Is there a link between inflation, interest rates and capital growth and, if so, what is it? Let's try to describe this connection so that we can then look at what might happen to property investment under changing conditions.

You can see that the 80s combination of high inflation, higher capital growth and even higher interest rates, while it still produced great returns for property investors, was "worse" than either the 60s or the 70s because of the relatively high cost of borrowing money. If we took this worst-case scenario to produce a reasonable combination of inflation, interest rates and capital growth, then the relationship would be:

Interest rates > capital growth > inflation

Using this worst-case scenario let's select a broad range of inflation rates (2%, 5%, 8% and 11%), and their respective combinations of capital growth and interest rates, so that we can analyse property under different inflationary regimes. These combinations are as follows:

Selected Combinations of Inflation, Capital Growth, and Interest Rates

Inflation	2.0%	5.0%	8.0%	11.0%
Capital Growth	4.5%	7.5%	11.5%	14.5%
Interest Rate	8.5%	10.0%	12.5%	15.0%

Many readers who have been unduly influenced by the media, may have difficulty accepting my contention that investing in property is still great, even with low inflation. Consequently, I have been very conservative in constructing the set of combinations for low inflation. For the lower rates of inflation, I have set the difference between inflation and capital growth at 2.5% (2% inflation with 4.5% capital growth, and 5% inflation with 7.5% capital growth), compared to a 3.5% difference for the two higher inflation rates of 8% and 11%. Also, I have recognised that with lower inflation, the banks increase their margin (the difference between inflation and interest rates). They can do this because of what they term "market toleration" — the market is more likely to accept an interest rate of 8.5% when inflation is 2% (a margin of 6.5%) compared to an interest rate of 15% when inflation is 11% (a margin of 4%).

Using the above set of rates, we are now in a position to compare the performance of property investment across the spectrum of low to high inflation. We want to see how inflation affects investment property in relation to the returns, the negative gearing benefits and the affordability. To simplify the process, I have used the computer program described on page 191 to produce a spreadsheet for each of the four combinations listed, and these are shown on the next two pages. Each spreadsheet is for our example $140,000 property as described on page 94.

Computer Projections at 2% Inflation

ASSUMPTIONS	Inputs	1yr	2yr	3yr	5yr	10yr
Property value	140,000	146,300	152,884	159,763	174,465	217,416
Purchase costs	4,000					
Deposit	0					
Loan	146,000	146,000	146,000	146,000	146,000	146,000
Equity	-6,000	300	6,884	13,763	28,465	71,416
Capital growth	**4.50%**	4.50%	4.50%	4.50%	4.50%	4.50%
Inflation rate	**2.00%**	2.00%	2.00%	2.00%	2.00%	2.00%
GROSS RENT /wk,/yr	180	9,360	9,547	9,738	10,132	11,186
CASH DEDUCTIONS						
Loan interest I/O	**8.50%**	12,410	12,410	12,410	12,410	12,410
Property expenses	25.00%	2,340	2,387	2,435	2,533	2,797
PRE-TAX CASH FLOW	0	-5,390	-5,250	-5,106	-4,811	-4,020
NON-CASH DEDUCTIONS						
Deprec.-building	2.50%	2,000	2,000	2,000	2,000	2,000
Deprec.-fittings	10,300	2,800	1,875	1,406	791	188
Borrowing costs	2,000	400	400	400	400	
TOTAL DEDUCTIONS	0	19,950	19,072	18,651	18,134	17,394
TAX CREDIT (actual)	44.40%	4,379	4,083	3,949	3,553	2,907
AFTER-TAX CASH FLOW	0	-1,011	-1,167	-1,157	-1,258	-1,113
RATE OF RETURN -IRR	**34.28%**		Your Cost Per Week			
Before-tax return	61.66%	19	22	22	24	21

Computer Projections at 5% Inflation

ASSUMPTIONS	Inputs	1yr	2yr	3yr	5yr	10yr
Property value	140,000	150,500	161,788	173,922	200,988	288,545
Purchase costs	4,000					
Deposit	0					
Loan	146,000	146,000	146,000	146,000	146,000	146,000
Equity	-6,000	4,500	15,788	27,922	54,988	142,545
Capital growth	**7.50%**	7.50%	7.50%	7.50%	7.50%	7.50%
Inflation rate	**5.00%**	5.00%	5.00%	5.00%	5.00%	5.00%
GROSS RENT /wk,/yr	180	9,360	9,828	10,319	11,377	14,520
CASH DEDUCTIONS						
Loan interest I/O	**10.00%**	14,600	14,600	14,600	14,600	14,600
Property expenses	25.00%	2,340	2,457	2,580	2,844	3,630
PRE-TAX CASH FLOW	0	-7,580	-7,229	-6,860	-6,067	-3,710
NON-CASH DEDUCTIONS						
Deprec.-building	2.50%	2,000	2,000	2,000	2,000	2,000
Deprec.-fittings	10,300	2,800	1,875	1,406	791	188
Borrowing costs	2,000	400	400	400	400	
TOTAL DEDUCTIONS	0	22,140	21,332	20,986	20,635	20,418
TAX CREDIT (actual)	44.40%	5,154	4,905	4,736	4,299	2,854
AFTER-TAX CASH FLOW	0	-2,426	-2,324	-2,124	-1,768	-856
RATE OF RETURN -IRR	**36.45%**		Your Cost Per Week			
Before-tax return	65.57%	47	45	41	34	16

Computer Projections at 8% Inflation

ASSUMPTIONS	Inputs	1yr	2yr	3yr	5yr	10yr
Property value	140,000	156,100	174,052	194,067	241,269	415,793
Purchase costs	4,000					
Deposit	0					
Loan	146,000	146,000	146,000	146,000	146,000	146,000
Equity	-6,000	10,100	28,052	48,067	95,269	269,793
Capital growth	**11.50%**	11.50%	11.50%	11.50%	11.50%	11.50%
Inflation rate	**8.00%**	8.00%	8.00%	8.00%	8.00%	8.00%
GROSS RENT /wk,/yr	180	9,360	10,109	10,918	12,734	18,711
CASH DEDUCTIONS						
Loan interest I/O	**12.50%**	18,250	18,250	18,250	18,250	18,250
Property expenses	25.00%	2,340	2,527	2,729	3,184	4,678
PRE-TAX CASH FLOW	0	-11,230	-10,668	-10,062	-8,699	-4,217
NON-CASH DEDUCTIONS						
Deprec.-building	2.50%	2,000	2,000	2,000	2,000	2,000
Deprec.-fittings	10,300	2,800	1,875	1,406	791	188
Borrowing costs	2,000	400	400	400	400	
TOTAL DEDUCTIONS	0	25,790	25,052	24,786	24,625	25,115
TAX CREDIT (actual)	44.40%	6,446	6,244	6,257	5,728	3,100
AFTER-TAX CASH FLOW	0	-4,784	-4,424	-3,805	-2,971	-1,117
RATE OF RETURN -IRR	**36.93%**		Your Cost	Per Week		
Before-tax return	66.43%	92	85	73	57	21

Computer Projections at 11% Inflation

ASSUMPTIONS	Inputs	1yr	2yr	3yr	5yr	10yr
Property value	140,000	160,300	183,544	210,157	275,521	542,229
Purchase costs	4,000					
Deposit	0					
Loan	146,000	146,000	146,000	146,000	146,000	146,000
Equity	-6,000	14,300	37,544	64,157	129,521	396,229
Capital growth	**14.50%**	14.50%	14.50%	14.50%	14.50%	14.50%
Inflation rate	**11.00%**	11.00%	11.00%	11.00%	11.00%	11.00%
GROSS RENT /wk,/yr	180	9,360	10,390	11,532	14,209	23,943
CASH DEDUCTIONS						
Loan interest I/O	**15.00%**	21,900	21,900	21,900	21,900	21,900
Property expenses	25.00%	2,340	2,597	2,883	3,552	5,986
PRE-TAX CASH FLOW	0	-14,880	-14,108	-13,251	-11,243	-3,943
NON-CASH DEDUCTIONS						
Deprec.-building	2.50%	2,000	2,000	2,000	2,000	2,000
Deprec.-fittings	10,300	2,800	1,875	1,406	791	188
Borrowing costs	2,000	400	400	400	400	
TOTAL DEDUCTIONS	0	29,440	28,772	28,589	28,643	30,074
TAX CREDIT (actual)	44.40%	7,738	7,583	7,791	6,987	2,967
AFTER-TAX CASH FLOW	0	-7,142	-6,525	-5,460	-4,256	-976
RATE OF RETURN -IRR	**37.16%**		Your Cost	Per Week		
Before-tax return	66.84%	137	125	105	82	19

Effect of Inflation on Returns

How do the different inflation rates, and their associated capital growth rates and interest rates affect the returns on your investment dollar? As I explained before, we need to relate the bottom line, which is your cost per week (after-tax cash flow), to the end result (equity) after any given period of time — in this case 10 years. The table below summarises these figures, as taken from the spreadsheets on the previous pages.

Effect of Inflation on Rate of Return (IRR)

Inflation	2.0%	5.0%	8.0%	11.0%
Capital Growth	4.5%	7.5%	11.5%	14.5%
Interest Rate	8.5%	10.0%	12.5%	15.0%
Cost/wk in 1st yr	$19	$47	$92	$137
Equity after 10yrs	$71,416	$142,545	$269,793	$396,229
Return (IRR)	34.28%	36.45%	36.93%	37.16%

First, let's look at these results on an "in-out" basis. When inflation is high (11%), interest rates are high (15%) and the after-tax cost is also high ($137 per week in the first year). Correspondingly, the equity after 10 years is high at $396,229. When inflation is low (2%), interest rates are low (8.5%), the after-tax cost is low ($19 per week in the first year), and likewise the equity after 10 years is low at $71,146. Can you see that as both inflation and interest rates fall, so does the cost per week?

It is a mistake to appraise the performance of property during high and low inflation by simply looking at the end result. It's easy for anyone to see that during high inflation and high capital growth, the equity achieved is greater than during low inflation and low capital growth. This is just stating the obvious. But a true property investment analysis must equally take into account the input dollars as well — and this is not as easy to see, nor as easy to calculate.

Using the computer, I have worked out the rate of return on the basis of all the "ins" and "outs" for each case. With inflation low at 2%, the rate of return is 34.28% per annum compound, while at the other end of the scale, with high inflation, the rate of return is 37.16% per annum compound. Compared to alternative investments, the difference between these rates of return is negligible, and consequently, *the different inflation rates have negligible effect on the rate of return*. But if you think that perhaps the rate is a little higher with higher inflation, let me go one step further. Let's look at the *real after-inflation* rate of return.

Don't Forget about the *Real* Effect of Inflation

Don't forget that, at the same time as you have been making a good return on your money through property investment, inflation is having an effect on what your money will buy. So, to compare different inflationary eras, we should convert the rates of return to *after-inflation* rates of return. The table below gives you the *real* rates of return, taking the inflation rate into account.

Effect of Inflation on Real Rate of Return (IRR after Inflation)

Inflation	2.0%	5.0%	8.0%	11.0%
Capital Growth	4.5%	7.5%	11.5%	14.5%
Interest Rate	8.5%	10.0%	12.5%	15.0%
Return (IRR)	34.28%	36.45%	36.93%	37.16%
Real Return (After Inflation)	31.64%	29.95%	26.78%	23.56%

(Note: The real return after inflation cannot be found by simply subtracting the inflation rate from the IRR. For those interested in technicalities, the formula is: $\{[(1 + IRR)/(1+Inflation)] - 1\}$. Otherwise, suffice to say that there is a small variation because the base money has grown in value by the inflation rate and the return must be divided by the new dollar value.)

There are several points to note here. First, if you look solely at the IRR, it appears as though there is a slightly better return from investment property during times of high inflation. With high inflation, the return is 37.16%, but if we reduce this return by inflation of 11%, we have a real return of 23.56%. On the other hand, when inflation is low at 2%, the return is 34.28%, and if we reduce this by the inflation rate, we have a real return of 31.64%! Without this mathematical explanation, intuitively you should realise that in times of high inflation, you need to get better returns in order to compensate for the devaluing of the dollar, compared to times of low inflation, where you can tolerate lower returns because the dollar is not devaluing as quickly.

From these analyses, you should now understand why the effect of inflation on property investment must be looked at in conjunction with the related factors of capital growth and interest rates. And while there is a link between these economic factors, I don't believe that low inflation, or high inflation or anything in between, makes any significant difference to the rates of return on investment property, as judged by the IRR.

Are these Returns Good?

We've just seen how the average annual rate of return from investment property can be higher than 20% per annum, despite the level of inflation. But are these returns really so good? Let's put these returns in perspective by comparing them to the returns from cash, shares and superannuation.

First, cash investments. Suppose that term deposit rates are 12% when inflation is 11% and that lending rates are 15%. If the investor's marginal tax rate was 40%, then the real rate of return would be:

Interest Rate on Term Deposit	= 12.0%	
Real After-Tax Rate of Return	= 7.2%	(12% less 40% of 12%)
After-Tax, After-Inflation Return	= - 3.4%	(Less inflation of 11%)

So with an interest rate of 12%, the "after everything" return is really minus 3.4%. The table below gives the after-tax, after-inflation returns for both property and cash, across a range of inflation rates. Interestingly, cash investments would produce a positive return only if inflation and interest rates were very low. Otherwise, the returns would be negative!

After-Tax, After-Inflation Returns from Rental Property and Cash Investments

Inflation	2.0%	5.0%	8.0%	11.0%
Borrowing Interest Rates	8.5%	10.0%	12.5%	15.0%
Cash Deposit Interest Rates	4.0%	6.0%	9.0%	12.0%
Returns from Property	31.6%	29.9%	26.7%	23.5%
Returns from Cash	.3%	- 1.3%	- 2.4%	- 3.4%

What about shares? I have already pointed out that, because of their volatility, it is difficult (and not wise) to gear highly into shares. Hence, investments in shares benefit little from gearing compared to residential property which can be highly and relatively safely negatively geared.

And superannuation? It is impossible to borrow money to invest into superannuation, and consequently, the returns are limited to the difference between inflation and capital growth, without the benefit of gearing. The historical after-tax, after-inflation returns from superannuation funds in Australia have been less than 3%! (Source: Report by Foster (1992) in "Economic and Social Consequences of Australia's Ageing Population")

When you compare the *real* returns from property to the *real* returns from other investments, then it's easy to understand why investing in property is so good at any time.

Effect of Inflation on -ve Gearing

Negative gearing is often seen as being in or out of fashion, depending on the size of the tax refund. The "fuzzy logic" here is that the higher the tax deductions, the bigger the tax refund, the better the performance of investment property.

Consequently, when tax refunds are smaller as a result of low inflation and low interest rates, many property investors believe that their "loss" of negative gearing benefits is bad for the performance of their investment. This apparent "loss" has led many investors to sell their property when, in fact, the most appropriate course of action was to buy more property. Let me give you an example.

In one particular instance, an investor was faced with a substantial reduction in his tax refund because of the fall in interest rates during 1992. The property, which he bought in 1988 for $85,000, had been highly geared. This resulted in a significant tax refund for many years when interest rates were particularly high (averaging 17%). The investor used his annual tax refund of about $5,000 to finance an overseas trip once a year for both him and his wife.

However, with the fall in interest rates to just 9% (he had a variable rate loan), his annual tax refund dropped to less than $1,000, such that he could no longer afford his annual overseas trip. At this point, he decided that the property was not performing as he had intended (i.e. to produce a tax refund) so he sold the property. With the money he made from the sale of the property, he took his entire family on an overseas holiday.

On his return, he decided to get back into negatively geared property, and found that with the lower interest rates, he could afford to borrow to buy a more expensive, but low yielding property for $300,000 — and once again he began to receive a handsome tax refund. He was happy (blissfully ignorant?), but I ask you — where is the logic?

He had failed to appreciate that although he was receiving a lower tax refund, the property was costing him less per week and he would have been saving far more than the tax refund was ever worth. Instead, he should have simply borrowed against the investment property to purchase more property, thereby increasing his overall return and restoring his annual tax-funded holiday. The costs of selling his original investment property (not to mention the CGT) and purchasing another one (the stamp duty alone was more than $8,000) made the overseas holiday a very expensive one.

This example is not an isolated case. Too many investors and advisors dwell on the tax refund, when they should be looking at the overall returns and the after-tax costs of the investment property.

Let's put tax refunds into perspective so that we can truly answer the question of whether or not negative gearing is dead or alive in times of low inflation and low interest rates. The table below shows the cost per week and the tax saving in the first year of an investment property. These figures have been taken from the spreadsheets on pages 122 and 123 and refer to our example $140,000 property that was detailed on page 94. The real return after inflation is also shown.

Effect of Inflation on Tax Savings

Inflation	2.0%	5.0%	8.0%	11.0%
Capital Growth	4.5%	7.5%	11.5%	14.5%
Interest Rate	8.5%	10.0%	12.5%	15.0%
Cost Per Week	$19	$47	$92	$137
Tax Saving	$4,379	$5,154	$6,446	$7,738
Real Return (After Inflation)	31.6%	29.9%	26.7%	23.5%

With 11% inflation and 15% interest rates, the tax refund would be high at $7,738 and likewise, the cost per week would be high at $137. However, with 2% inflation and 8.5% interest rates, the tax refund would be low at just $4,379 — a reduction of more than $3,000 — but the weekly cost to the investor would also be low at $19. In fact, in times of low inflation and low interest rates, it is possible to be negatively geared with a positive cash flow, and we will look at this later in the Appendix.

Isn't it better to pay less per week for an investment property and get a better return (31.6% compared to 23.5%), than to simply aim for a big tax refund? Tax refunds are just the icing on the cake to an already great investment. If you want to maintain the same level of tax refund, you need only to increase your borrowings to invest in more property.

Low inflation, low interest rates, and low tax refunds do NOT affect the investment returns from negatively geared property, and looking at just the *size* of the tax refund is like looking through a keyhole — you only see half the picture.

You must also remember the *real* reason as to why you are negatively geared — and that is to increase the returns on your investment dollar enabling you to retire sooner and wealthier, not because you want a big fat tax refund. In the previous chapter, you saw how Bill and Mary could borrow to buy property over a 10 year period. Let's look at what would have happened if Bill and Mary had decided *not* to negatively gear.

Suppose that Bill and Mary decided to save their money and invest it in term deposits so that they could eventually pay cash for their investment property. The table below shows what would happen if the contributions earmarked for property (position 9 in the table on page 101) were invested in a term deposit at 6% (3.6% after tax at a 40% tax rate). The cumulative total of their savings plus interest is shown on the right of the table and the increasing value of the example $140,000 property is on the left.

Saving to Buy an Investment Property

Year	Property Value	Contribution (Savings)	Interest on Savings	Cumulative Cash Total
0	$140,000	$5,658	$204	$5,862
1	$150,500	$21,034	$968	$27,864
2	$161,788	$18,955	$1,685	$48,504
3	$173,922	$26,778	$2,710	$77,993
4	$186,966	$24,067	$3,674	$105,734
5	$200,988	$21,214	$4,570	$131,518
6	$216,062	$31,336	$5,863	$168,717
7	$232,267	$27,705	$7,071	$203,493
8	$249,687	$23,885	$8,186	$235,563
9	$268,413	$36,966	$9,811	$282,340
10	$288,544	$32,191	$11,323	$325,855

If Bill and Mary had NOT borrowed money and were NOT negatively geared, it would have taken them more than 9 years to save up to buy just one property! At that point, they would have saved $282,340, enough to pay cash for one investment property valued at $268,413. The reason it takes forever to save up enough to pay cash for a property is that no matter how fast you save, the interest earned is being chewed up by tax, and the property is increasing in value every year, putting it further out of reach. And what if Bill and Mary had decided to gear to a break even point by saving for half and borrowing the rest? It would still have taken them more than 4 years to accumulate half the value of the property!

Compare these results to the more than $600,000 in net worth that Bill and Mary would have achieved by negative gearing (see Year 9 of the table on page 101) and you will realise that gearing increases the rate of return, hastens the rate at which you can buy property, and decreases the time you need to invest for your retirement!

Effect of Inflation on Affordability

The real cost of purchasing an investment property can vary depending on the prevailing inflation and interest rates. One of the side effects of low inflation, and consequently low interest rates, is the low cost of borrowing money, which makes buying an investment property even more affordable. An investor is able to purchase more property (either a property of a greater value or a greater number of properties) for the same cost.

Financial institutions use a fairly standard formula for calculating the affordability. No matter how much equity you have in your properties, the bottom line for banks is your ability to service the loan — in other words — can you afford the repayments? In most cases, the substantial tax savings are not taken into account and neither is the spouse's total income. (It is assumed that the second income is not a fully disposable amount that could easily be put towards loan payments.)

Consequently, the general formula is just a simple comparison between total incomings (wages and rent) and total outgoings (loan payments). In a situation where an investor was earning $45,000 per year, the spouse was earning $6,000 per year, and they bought our example $140,000 property that could be rented for $9,360 per year, the affordability according to a financial institution's calculation would be:

Applying a Financial Institution's Affordability Calculation

Affordability	=	30% of Income	+	80% of Rent
	=	30% of $51,000	+	80% of $9,360
	=	$15,300	+	$7,488
	=	$22,788		
	=	must be greater than the total loan payments		

This means that the total loan payments for this investor must not exceed $22,788. In the case where there are no other loan payments (e.g. for a housing loan for a principal place of residence, or a personal loan for a car, new kitchen, etc.), the total loan payments would relate only to the investment property. Also, with an interest-only loan, the loan payments would be just the interest component.

With a fixed limit of affordability at $22,788 for this investor, we can now see how it would be affected by the different interest rates in times of changing inflation. If the varying interest payments are isolated from the four spreadsheets relating to our example property on pages 122 and 123, we can easily compare the differences in affordability for those different rates. The figures for affordability level and interest payments are shown in the table below.

Effect of Inflation on Affordability

Inflation	2.0%	5.0%	8.0%	11.0%
Capital Growth	4.5%	7.5%	11.5%	14.5%
Interest Rate	8.5%	10.0%	12.5%	15.0%
Affordability	$22,788	$22,788	$22,788	$22,788
Interest	$12,410	$14,600	$18,250	$21,900
Debt Service	Very Easy	Easy	Comfortable	Barely

For high inflation (11%) and interest payments of $21,900 (15% of $146,000), you would barely qualify for one investment property! In fact, high interest rates exclude many investors from the property market. For example, a couple with a joint income of just under the $51,000 used here would not qualify for a loan on this example property.

However, with lower inflation (8%) and lower interest rates (12.5%), the affordability becomes much more comfortable, with interest payments at $18,250. With even lower inflation of 2%, and interest payments of just $12,410, one investment property is very easily affordable. Indeed, with low inflation and low interest rates, you might even think about buying two or more properties.

Let's now look at the overall impact of property investment in different inflationary environments. Remember I said that you cannot compare the amount of money made during high inflation to that made during lower inflation and that it had to be related back to the actual money put into the property — i.e. we had to compare the "ins" and the "outs"? Well, let's do this in a slightly different way so that you can see once and for all why low inflation does not kill property as an investment. We'll not only look at the returns, but also the amount made from property in *today's dollars,* taking into account the number of properties that can be afforded as a result of the different interest rates.

Let's reconsider the example $140,000 property in each of the four different inflationary environments. First, we'll look at how many of these properties can be afforded in each situation. And just to make sure that I'm on the conservative side, I'll use the bank's standard formula for calculating affordability, without taking into account the tax savings from negative gearing. These calculations are shown on the following page.

Number of Properties Able to be Bought
(Using Bank's Affordability Calculation)

(1)   2% Inflation, 8.5% Interest Rate (3 Properties)

= 30% of Income   +   80% of Rent from 3 properties

= $15,300   + $22,464

= $37,764

> $37,230 (Interest Payments)

In this case the income of $37,764 is greater than the interest payment of $37,230, and three properties could be afforded.

(2)   5% Inflation, 10% Interest Rate (2 Properties)

= 30% of Income   +   80% of Rent from 2 properties

= $15,300   + $14,976

= $30,276

> $29,200 (Interest Payments)

In this case the income of $30,276 is greater than the interest payment of $29,200, and two properties could be afforded.

(3)   8% Inflation, 12.5% Interest Rate (1 Property)

= 30% of Income   +   80% of Rent from 1 property

= $15,300   + $7,488

= $22,788

> $18,250 (Interest Payments)

In this case the income of $22,788 is greater than the interest payment of $18,250, and only one property could be afforded.

(4)   11% Inflation, 15% Interest Rate (1 Property)

= 30% of Income   +   80% of Rent from 1 property

= $15,300   + $7,488

= $22,788

> $21,900 (Interest Payments)

In this case the income of $22,788 is greater than the interest payment of $21,900, and only one property could be afforded — but just barely.

As you can see from the affordability table on the previous page, with low interest rates of 8.5% it would be possible to buy three properties; with interest rates at 10%, two could be afforded, and with higher rates, only one could be afforded. The next step is to make some comparisons between what you put in, and the "real" money that you get out, taking inflation into account. The table below shows the results for the different combinations of inflation, capital growth and interest rates.

It gives information on the number of properties able to be bought, the cost per week in the first year for one property, the cost per week in the first year for the total number of properties able to be afforded, and the equity after 10 years for the properties. It also gives the selling costs and Capital Gains Tax, the net profit after sale at 10 years, and the real value of this profit in today's dollars, taking into account inflation.

"Real" Money Made with Changing Inflation Rates

Inflation	2.0%	5.0%	8.0%	11.0%
Capital Growth	4.5%	7.5%	11.5%	14.5%
Interest Rate	8.5%	10.0%	12.5%	15.0%
Properties able to be afforded	3	2	1	1
Cost/wk (1st yr) for 1 property	$19	$47	$92	$137
Cost/wk (1st yr) for all properties	$103 (3)	$108 (2)	$92 (1)	$137 (1)
Original value of 1 property	$140,000	$140,000	$140,000	$140,000
Value of 1 property after 10 yrs	$217,416	$288,544	$415,793	$542,229
Original loan on 1 property	$146,000	$146,000	$146,000	$146,000
Equity in 1 property after 10yrs	$71,416	$142,545	$269,793	$396,229
Total equity after 10 years	$214,247	$285,089	$269,793	$396,229
Selling costs and CGT	$66,890	$61,422	$57,444	$73,168
Profit after selling costs + CGT	$147,357	$223,667	$212,349	$323,061
Net profit (in today's dollars)	$120,893	$137,320	$98,359	$113,777
Real Return on all Properties (After inflation, after tax, after selling costs and after CGT)	18.1%	23.5%	22.9%	20.4%

With 11% inflation, one property would cost $137 per week in the first year, dropping to $19 by the 10th year. At the end of 10 years, the total equity would be $396,229. If the selling costs and Capital Gains Tax amounted to $73,168, then the net equity would be $323,061. Bringing this back to today's dollars by taking inflation into account, this would result in a net profit of $113,777, giving us an after-sale, after-tax, after-inflation return of 20.4% on the cash flows outlaid.

At the other end of the scale, with inflation low at just 2%, it would be possible to buy three properties at a total cost of $103 per week in the first year, dropping to $75 per week by the 10th year. (Note that the initial weekly cost of three properties is not three times $19, which is the initial weekly cost of one property. This is because with each extra property purchased, the additional tax deductions bring the taxable income down into the lower marginal tax rates, resulting in a slightly lower tax refund and a slightly higher cost.)

After 10 years of low inflation (2%), the equity in each of the three properties would be $71,416, giving a total equity of $214,247. Taking into account the selling costs and Capital Gains Tax totalling $66,890, the net equity would be $147,357, which, if converted back to today's dollars, would be $120,893. This would give us an after-sale, after-tax, after-inflation return of 18.1% on the three properties!

Across the entire range of inflation rates, the after-everything return for 10 years does *not* vary greatly at all, and no one could possibly say that low or high inflation is better or worse for property investors. So let's get rid of the myth that low inflation kills property as an investment. No matter what the inflation rate, the returns from property in the long term can be so good that they can multiply your net worth more quickly and more safely than any other investment.

11

Government Changes are Taxing

Governments at all levels, Federal, State and Local, can devise and implement policies that affect property investors. Policy changes, such as those that have resulted in the creation of the Rental Bond Board and the introduction of the Tenancy Acts, affect both tenants and landlords. But usually such changes only affect the amount of time spent filling in forms rather than the amount of money spent by the investor.

However, it is in the area of taxation that policy changes most affect the hip pocket of property investors. The major taxation areas that affect property investors are the tax deductions and personal tax rates, both of which can affect the tax refund available to negatively geared property investors, and capital taxes such as the familiar Capital Gains Tax.

First, when investors think of tax deductions for investment property, they usually think of negative gearing. This is the situation that occurs when the total tax deductions exceed the rent, creating a loss which usually results in a tax refund. Because the loan interest is the major tax deduction causing the loss, it is this negative gearing component that is sometimes in the firing line of potential taxation changes. Having tampered with the "negative gearing" element before, is the Government likely to tamper with it in the foreseeable future?

Secondly, both major political parties have policies aimed at lowering personal tax rates in favour of increasing the indirect tax base. This leaves property investors wondering what the impact might be on the tax benefits and returns from negatively geared property.

And thirdly, any tax that affects the capital of an asset is viewed by the majority of investors as a "wealth tax" in disguise. What are these capital taxes and how do they affect property investors? Moreover, are there any new ones on the horizon? Let's look at these three areas of taxation to see what changes have already occurred, and are proposed, so that we can gauge how such changes might affect property investors.

Negative Gearing under Siege

Governments have continued to reduce the number of tax deductions available to average wage earners, who can now claim little more than a rubber and a ruler as legitimate expenses. Gone are the long lists of tax writeoffs that allowed most workers to receive an end-of-year tax refund that at least covered the cost of the accountant.

So it is understandable that many investors have a high regard for the tax deductions available to property investors, particularly the highly prized "negative gearing" interest deduction. However, many investors have wrongly viewed this tax concession as the sole reason for investing in property, as events of the mid-1980s proved.

In 1985, the then Labor Government abolished the right to offset the interest on an investment property loan against other income. (All other expenses were still available as a deduction, and losses could be carried forward to when the property was cash positive.) It was seen as a way of getting rid of property *speculators* and in doing so, saving the Government money by reducing the size of the tax refund owing to property *investors*.

At the time, the Government must have been aware that it needed to offer an alternative incentive to investors so that they would continue to buy rental property. So they simultaneously introduced a capital allowance of 4% on the construction cost of new buildings, which could be directly offset against other income. By encouraging property investors to buy new buildings, the introduction of the capital allowance on residential property was also designed to stimulate the housing industry.

The Government, however, completely misread the psychology of the investor. Despite the seemingly attractive 4% capital allowance on new buildings, the result was that investors shied away from investing in property.

Unfortunately for the Government, the people most affected by these tax changes were not the investors, but the tenants. The lack of property investors resulted in a shortage of rental properties and rents skyrocketed. In some of the capital cities, rents almost doubled and the tenant backlash was much greater than the Government had ever anticipated.

In New South Wales alone, there was an increase of almost 40% in the number of people on the waiting list for public housing between 1985 and 1987. Suddenly the Government became aware that taxation benefits to investors play an extremely important part in assisting with the provision of housing to a large section of the population. Tax incentives encourage investors to buy rental property, and this reduces the number of tenants dependent on public housing.

So great was the tenant backlash that the legislation was reversed two years later in 1987, with full deductibility being restored to investors. The Government's stated reasons for this complete about face were that the Capital Gains Tax was now acting as a sufficient deterrent to property speculators and that the cost of paying additional tax refunds to negatively geared investors would now be offset by the CGT. With the reintroduction of the negative gearing deduction, investors were once again lured back into property investment. The chart below graphically shows the rise and fall in the number of people waiting on the public housing list in New South Wales, the time of increase and decrease in numbers clearly coinciding with the abolition and reintroduction of negative gearing.

Tenants Affected by Abolition of Negative Gearing

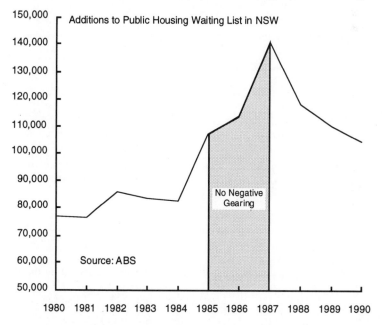

If we look overseas, you will better understand the role of negative gearing in our public housing system. All countries subsidise their public housing. They do it either by direct rental assistance, or by providing subsidised land and buildings, or by providing tax incentives to the private sector. Most of the European countries, particularly the socialist ones, fund their public housing directly, rather than relying on tax incentives to the private sector. Consequently, they have more than 20% of their populations relying on Government provided accommodation.

In contrast, in Australia, where the subsidy comes mostly in the form of tax incentives to the private sector, less than 8% of the population rely on public housing, while the remaining 22% rent from the private sector. (Currently in Australia, about 30% of the population rent.) It is obvious that there is a great need for rental accommodation in Australia, but it would require huge capital outlays, money that the Government doesn't have, to reverse the method of subsidy. The Government has apparently rationalised that it is cheaper and more effective to subsidise the private sector (through tax incentives) to provide rental housing.

Having shown you the rationale for retaining the negative gearing laws, would it be possible for Governments to once again abolish them? Both political parties have stated that they are *"committed to the retention of negative gearing in its present form"*. However, you must realise that we are dealing with politicians whose "promises" are often victims of political expediency. Let's have a look at what *could* happen if the Government did abolish the right to claim losses from rental property against other income. In other words, suppose that tax refunds from investment property were non existent as of now. What would you do?

If you were to do like most investors did between 1985 and 1987, you'd probably look around for some investment other than property that offered more attractive tax advantages. Perhaps emu farms or pine plantations? And do you know what would happen then? Just like the 80s, there would probably be a rental property shortage followed by massive hikes in rent due to the supply and demand situation created by more tenants chasing fewer properties. (After negative gearing was abolished in 1985, rental yields were extremely high, averaging 10%.)

If we analysed this situation, you would see the folly of believing that tax deductibility of interest is the cornerstone of property investment. The overall long-term rate of return from investment property would not be significantly affected because the loss of tax benefits would be compensated for by the increase in rental yields.

One further point. In the event that the negative gearing laws were tampered with, it would be highly unlikely that they would be made retrospective (the laws were not made retrospective in 1985). So anyone who already owned negatively geared property should be able to continue with their existing claims regardless.

If the Government were to abolish negative gearing today, we would be the first to buy more investment property because we understand the herd mentality of many investors. Between 1985 and 1987, when this scenario last occurred, we continued to borrow to buy property as though nothing had happened.

Changes in Personal Tax Rates

With both the Liberal and Labor Parties favouring indirect taxation the way is open for a reduction in personal tax rates, and naturally this leaves many investors wondering whether negative gearing will be worthwhile or not. Already, in 1994, there has been a lowering of personal tax rates, and further reductions are proposed for 1996, although many commentators question whether or not these proposed changes will actually eventuate. (Yet another one of the Government's "promises" to bite the dust?)

What is the effect of lowered personal tax rates on property investment?

First, let's look closely at the rates that existed in the early 90s, together with those introduced in 1994 and those proposed for 1996, so that you can see just where the changes have been made, and *may* be made in the future. The tax rates for the various income brackets are shown in the table below.

Tax Scales for 1992, 1994 and 1996 (Proposed)

1992 Old	Rate (%)	1994 Current	Rate (%)	1996 Proposed	Rate (%)
0 - 5,400	0	0 - 5,400	0	0 - 5,400	0
5,401 - 20,700	20	5,401 - 20,700	20	5,401 - 20,700	20
20,701 - 36,000	38	20,701 - 38,000	34	20,701 - 40,000	30
36,001 - 50,000	46	38,001 - 50,000	43	40,001 - 50,000	40
50,001+	47	50,001 +	47	50,001+	47

There are several things to note. First, there has been no proposal to introduce a flat tax rate, and all the above tax scales are graduated. The higher marginal tax rates for higher income levels mean that the more you earn, the more tax you pay in terms of the percentage of the dollar earned, and extra income is taxed at these higher marginal rates. For those property investors who are negatively geared, this has a very favourable effect as "losses" are taken off the top of incomes and therefore tax savings are also at the higher marginal rates.

The marginal tax rates of 30 to 40 cents in the dollar are not exactly insignificant levels (with more than one third of overtime for the average worker disappearing in tax) and these rates begin to cut in at a relatively low income level of $20,700. Hence, low to average income earners still benefit from negative gearing by receiving tax benefits that are calculated at rates of at least 30 cents in the dollar.

The top marginal rates (for incomes of over $40,000) do not vary substantially between the old and new rates. I am talking about only a few cents in the dollar difference between the top rates in all years, and consequently, for negatively geared property investors, the tax savings would not be substantially altered — certainly not enough to warrant the abandonment of negative gearing.

But by far the most important point is that by 1996, when (or if) the new rates will apply, most wage earners will be earning more income either through natural increases due to inflation, or career promotions, and thus many of them will have moved back into the higher rates through bracket creep. Let's look at how bracket creep affects a typical wage earner so that you will understand why the Government's new tax rates are not what they appear to be. Take the case of Bill who, in 1994, earns $45,000 per year, and buys the example investment property for $140,000 (see page 94). How would the new tax rates affect his investment in property?

Let's suppose that in 1992, Bill earned $41,000 per year and that by the year 1996, he is expected to be earning $49,000 per year. This assumes that his wages increase at approximately 5% per year over the four years. The table below gives you the "cost per week" figure (in the first year) and also the annual rate of return over 10 years, for each of the tax scales.

The Effect of Bracket Creep
on Negatively Geared Investment Property

	1992 Old	1994 Current	1996 Proposed
Tax Refund	$5,435	$5,154	$4,913
Cost/wk in 1st yr	$41	$47	$50
Rate of Return (IRR)	38.06%	36.45%	36.26%

The effect of bracket creep, is that, although Bill's marginal tax rates are decreasing over the years, his income is carried into the higher rates by wage increases, and the tax refund would vary by only a few hundred dollars over the years. The result is that the investment property bought by Bill would have cost him $41 per week in 1992, with a return of 38.06%, $47 per week in 1994 with a return of 36.45% and $50 in 1996 with a return of 36.26%. These differences are negligible to say the least and would not have affected Bill in his plan to build wealth through investment property.

One other point must be mentioned. Everything is relative. And if personal tax rates are lowered, then all other investments relying on tax effectiveness would be similarly affected.

The Future of Wealth Taxes

Property investors seem to accept that Governments can tamper with either the personal tax rates, or the tax deductibility of some expenses, such as the interest on negatively geared property. It is generally accepted, with some reluctance, that income taxes are a necessary evil. But taxation of capital accrued in property is often seen as a thinly disguised wealth tax, which is unpalatable to the majority of the electorate. The belief is that such wealth taxes infringe on the rights of a person to own and accumulate possessions. Moreover, wealth taxes take away from you money that you already *have*, compared to income taxes where the money is taken away from you *before* you get to *see* it. In Australia, taxes on the capital value of property are levied as a result of buying, owning or selling property and can be imposed by all levels of Government at the Federal, State or Local Government level. Below is a list of such taxes.

Capital (Wealth) Taxes on Property

Government Level	Capital Tax	Time of Tax
Local	Rates	During ownership
State	Stamp Duty on Title	At purchase
State	Land Tax	During ownership
Federal	Capital Gains Tax	On selling
Federal	Inheritance Tax (?)	On death

Let's look at these taxes in more detail, together with another tax that has been lurking in the background for some time — the inheritance tax.

Local Government Taxes

Rates

Although rates usually include a standard levy for essential services such as water, sewage, and garbage disposal, a large percentage of rates is based on the property value, and therefor represents a form of wealth tax. With Local Governments becoming responsible for more and more "grass roots" services, it is highly likely that the system will remain intact in Australia, particularly in view of the experience in the United Kingdom. Margaret Thatcher attempted to take away the "wealth tax" element from rates by introducing a Poll Tax, which essentially was a form of rates where everyone paid the same amount regardless of their property holdings. The public outcry was so loud that Margaret eventually lost her job and all attempts to introduce this tax were quickly abandoned.

State Government Taxes

Land Tax

I couldn't count the number of times people have told me that they are not going to buy investment property because they will have to pay too much land tax. But by the time you have accumulated sufficient properties to qualify you for it, you can probably well afford it.

Land tax is a capital tax based on the unimproved value of the land. It is a State-levied tax and each State has different rates and rules. They all have exemptions of one form or another that may or may not include the principal place of residence.

Land tax can be minimised in several ways. First, buying property in several States would reduce the tax payable in each State. This should not be seen as an incentive to spread properties around Australia, but more of an added bonus if property is purchased interstate. The second method relates to the ownership of the property. In some States, land tax can be minimised by carefully selecting the name in which the property is to be purchased. However, at the same time, this may interfere with the tax refund available to negatively geared property investors.

For example, in Queensland land tax can be minimised by buying investment properties in joint names because each person is entitled to a threshold of $160,000. However, this may affect the tax refund available to a couple who have negatively geared property and where one partner is not working. On the other hand, in NSW, the land tax threshold applies to the partnership, not the individual within the partnership. The properties are then best bought in single names, in which case each person has the benefit of a threshold limit. Sounds confusing? It is very confusing, as any land tax officer will tell you. The important point is that measures taken to minimise land tax should be carefully considered in conjunction with measures to maximise negative gearing benefits.

No matter where you live, or in which State you buy property, land tax is considered to be a legitimate tax deduction for property investors, as it is an expense that is incurred during the process of producing income. Consequently, the effect of the tax is minimal and has little effect on the overall returns from investment property. (See pages 174 and 175 for a more detailed analysis.)

There have been several unsuccessful attempts to abolish land tax in Australia (in the early 1990s, the then Premier of NSW, Mr Nick Greiner, attempted to abolish it during his term of office, but did not succeed), but it appears as though it is firmly entrenched in the State systems. My own philosophy is that land tax is a part and parcel of investing in property and is an insufficient burden to be regarded as a deterrent.

Stamp Duty

Stamp duty is another State-levied tax and is based on the purchase price of a property. It is a once-off tax which is not tax deductible, but is taken into account in assessing the CGT payable on the sale of property.

The cost of the stamp duty can be built into the initial loan for an investment property, and therefore the interest on the extra borrowings is tax deductible. However, the logistics of paying this tax can often leave property investors in a Catch 22 situation. Although the stamp duty can be borrowed, financial institutions insist that it must be paid *prior* to the settlement date of the property, and of course the loan monies are not available until settlement date.

One simple solution is to borrow on credit card to pay the stamp duty, and repay the "loan" immediately on receiving the extra funds at settlement. Alternatively, the financial institution may be willing to advance the cost before settlement date.

With stamp duty firmly imbedded in the States' taxation system, this tax is here to stay and if anything, is likely to increase in the future. On average, stamp duty represents about 20% of the taxes collected by State Governments. And with the States receiving less and less Federal funding, they are being forced to increase their own tax base. As a result, stamp duty has increased in all States in recent years and like it or not, this trend is likely to continue.

Federal Government Taxes

Capital Gains Tax

Capital Gains Tax was introduced on September 19, 1985, and applies to all assets acquired after that time with a few, but notable exceptions, such as the family home. It was never intended that the tax should strip property investors of their assets, but rather to tax them on the sale of assets on which they had made "excessive" gains. As such, it applies to only that part of the capital gain that is over and above inflation, and it is a lesser tax than had the entire gain been taxed at the investor's marginal rate. The tax should actually encourage investors to keep, rather than to sell their properties. Indeed, this was the intention of the Federal Government at the time of its introduction.

The Capital Gains Tax is now a firmly entrenched tax and there is little likelihood that it will be abolished. In fact, while the CGT remains intact, I believe there is little or no likelihood of the Federal Government tampering with the negative gearing laws. There are many ways in which property investors can minimise the CGT, and these were discussed in detail on page 112.

Inheritance   Tax?

Australia is one of the few countries in the industrialised world that currently does not have either an inheritance or a gift tax. These two taxes are linked because in an effort to avoid inheritance tax, people may gift assets to heirs prior to death. Victoria, in 1984, was the last Australian State to phase out these death-related taxes. What is the chance that such taxes will be reintroduced? With a growing budget deficit linked to an ageing population, the temptation for our Governments is obvious.

In Chapter 3, I mentioned that there was a strong possibility that it would be your grandchildren who would be paying the extra taxes necessary to fund the pensions of our future retirees. But if this younger generation rebel loudly and long enough, Governments could be forced to search for funds in other directions. Already, inheritance taxes have been identified as an alternative source of retirement funding. In a submission to the Federal Government in March, 1994, the Australian Pensioners and Superannuants Federation called for the introduction of an inheritance tax to fund higher pensions and services for older people.

The experience in other countries with an inheritance tax is that the tax represents an average of 1% of the total taxes collected. However, Canada abolished its death-related taxes because the gross yield from the taxes was equivalent to the collection costs, and wealthy Canadians never paid the taxes anyway. (Source: *Personal Investment*, September, 1993)

In Australia, although there is no inheritance or gift tax, the Capital Gains Tax accounts for almost 1% of taxes. Many have argued that the CGT is a quasi-death tax, because most of the taxes collected via the CGT have been paid as a result of beneficiaries of estates on-selling their inheritances. If the Government were ever to introduce an inheritance and gift tax, I believe that it must be done in conjunction with a modification of the CGT. Otherwise, we will face a situation where Australians pay double death taxes — once when they inherit property, and again in the form of the CGT when they are forced to sell the property to pay for the inheritance tax.

On a lighter note, I also believe that you should not be too concerned about death taxes (or inheritance taxes, depending on your point of view), as I am a great believer in building wealth with the ultimate aim of enjoying it while you can. Yes, you can think of wealth partly as a means of "getting the children started", but most people who inherit wealth do not know how to look after it, and experience has shown that inherited wealth is quickly "redistributed" — one generation makes it while the next spends it. So does it really matter whether or not the wealth is redistributed by the Government or by your heirs?

12
The Human Factor

Analysing investment property in light of future economic and political changes is a relatively easy exercise that simply involves plugging figures into a mathematical model to gauge the outcome. One factor is often forgotten in such an analysis, however, and this is the "human factor".

No matter how well educated we are, human nature seems to dictate the way we think and act, and, as a result, many of our day to day decisions revolve around the "human factor". How many times have you followed the rush of people to a flashing red light in a shop and bought that "special bargain" in the heat of the moment, only to find out later that you could have bought the same item even more cheaply two aisles over in the same shop? At the time, we associate "rushing people" and "flashing red lights" with bargains, but when we have time to look around and assess the real situation, we realise that logic has been overtaken by "lemmingitis".

Property investors are no different and often make illogical assumptions based on irrational interpretations of the facts. They hear that the rate of population growth in Australia is slowing and assume that there will be a reduced demand for property in the future with lower capital growth. They read about the mass movements of people from the south to the north of Australia and so assume that Queensland property will produce the greatest capital growth. They see that interest rates have fallen to record lows, and assume that all tenants will be wanting to buy their own home, resulting in too few tenants. They notice that many people are buying books (like this one) on property and see a lot of advertisements for negative gearing seminars and they assume that everyone will be buying property, with a seeming resultant oversupply of rental properties.

But is there any truth to these assumptions?

Let's look at the facts behind these casual observations, to see just how important the "human factor" is in property investment. First we'll look at the population trends and the movement of people both in and around Australia. Then we'll examine the conjecture that there will be too few tenants and too many property investors.

Population Trends

According to projections by the United Nations, BIS Shrapnel and the Australian Bureau of Statistics, Australia's population is likely to increase at more than 1.5% compound annually over the next few decades, levelling out at 1% towards the middle of the 21st century. This will be the result of natural increase and also immigration, almost 60% of the increase being caused by the latter.

At these rates of increase, the population, currently 17.6 million, will surpass 26 million by the year 2031, and will be 30 million by the year 2051. The graph below vividly shows how Australia's population has increased from 1861 to 1994, and what the envisaged increase will be over the next fifty years.

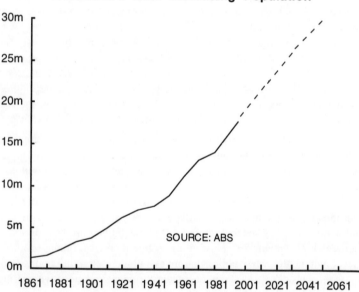

Australia's Ever Increasing Population

SOURCE: ABS

The continued increases will place great demands on housing in the future. But just as important as the overall increase in population, is the direction of movement of people both in and around Australia. First, people move between rural and urban areas. Secondly, interstate migration affects some States more favourably than others. And thirdly, immigrants from overseas do not spread themselves equally around the country.

Urbanisation

For better or for worse, Australia is following the European trend of people moving away from the rural countryside and into more urban areas (towns of more than 2,500 people) as shown in the table below.

In 1851, more than half (60%) of Australia's population lived in rural areas, but over the past century this has gradually decreased, and by 1991 was only 14%. One of the key factors precipitating this trend has been the mechanisation of the farming industry, with the resultant reduction in the need for farm labourers.

The Urbanisation of the Population

	1851	1891	1921	1991
Urban	40%	50%	62%	86%
Rural	60%	50%	38%	14%

Source: ABS

This urbanisation trend has very important implications for property investors. Obviously, capital growth of property depends to a large extent on continued demand and therefore it would be wise to invest in a city or town where the population is increasing. Most of the major cities and provincial towns in Australia today fit this bill — particularly if they have a broad industry base.

But be wary of towns based on a single unstable industry. For example, a gold mining town in outback Queensland once boasted 100 pubs and a population of almost 40,000 in its hey day of more than 60 years ago. Today, the population is just 10,000 with only 10 pubs, and relies largely on tourism.

Interstate Migration

People move interstate for all sorts of reasons, such as better climate, better employment prospects, or better facilities. Queensland, with its catchy slogan "beautiful one day, perfect the next" has attracted many "southerners". And likewise, with their own warmer climates, Western Australia and the Northern Territory, have also attracted many interstate migrants.

The result is that these particular States are often singled out as better places to invest. However, as I'll show you, looking at the figures for interstate migration alone does not give a true picture of population trends in Australia.

Immigration from Overseas

Australia has always been a favoured destination for immigrants from overseas with net migration averaging 100,000 annually, depending on the political and economic conditions at the time. During slow economic times immigration is reduced, while during boom times, the Government's immigration program is stepped up to allow for the intake of skilled workers in demand by thriving industries. This pattern was typified during the 1984 "recession" when net immigration was about 44,000, as opposed to the 1989 "boom", when net immigration exceeded 123,000.

However, it is the destination of these immigrants that is significant. For while there is a net movement of people within Australia out of the southern States of Victoria and New South Wales and into the warmer States such as Queensland, both of these southern States are the prime destinations for immigrants from overseas. Let's look at the figures for these States so that you will understand why it is misleading to look at *only* the internal migratory patterns. I have chosen to look at just these three States simply because they are highly representative of why you must look at the whole picture — not because I have forgotten about the other states. The table below gives the figures for the numbers of people who have either moved into or out of Victoria, New South Wales and Queensland over the past 10 years.

10 Yrs of Interstate Migration and Overseas Immigration (NSW, Vic, and Qld)

	Vic	NSW	Qld
Net Interstate Migration	-127,000	-168,100	295,100
Net Overseas Immigration	296,300	462,700	134,400
Net Intake	**169,300**	**294,600**	**429,500**

As you can see, Queensland is a target State of "southerners", with a net interstate intake of 295,100 people. However, because of the "human factor", most overseas immigrants prefer to move to the southern States of New South Wales and Victoria, where they can be close to their "already-settled" family and friends. As a result, almost 800,000 people have immigrated to these southern States in the past 10 years.

Yes, Queensland's net intake from interstate and overseas is higher than that of the other States, but any small change in immigration patterns could easily upset this balance. So if you are looking for population growth as a criterion for choosing the best place for investment, you must look at the whole picture, not just interstate movements.

The map below shows the circuitous route of people moving into Australia through the southern States, with others moving from the southern States to the north and west.

Pattern of Interstate Migration and Overseas Immigration

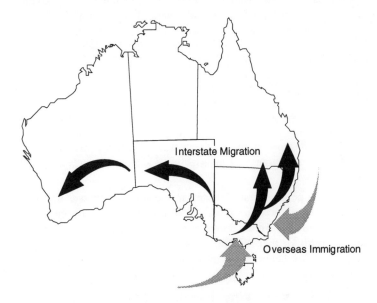

But perhaps the one factor that could not only increase Australia's population beyond all expectations, but could also tip the balance of net State population increases, has yet to be accounted for. With world-wide unrest, refugees are ever increasing in numbers — and Australia is a prime target. An article in the *Courier Mail*, July 1993, exposed the likelihood of Australia being on the receiving end of massive migrations of people due to the increasing numbers of dispossessed people. The article stated:

The United Nations warned Australia last night to be prepared for a flood of refugees and migrants as the world population explodes.

... population and environmental pressures would lead to unprecedented numbers seeking new homes and improved lifestyles in relatively wealthy countries.

Should anyone have any doubts about the projections for Australia's population, they need only look at this mounting refugee problem to realise that, like it or not, Australia may soon be pressured to open its gates to the rest of the world, placing unprecedented demands on housing.

Too Few Tenants?

Many property investors question whether there will be a continuing supply of tenants in the future. Lower interest rates enable more tenants to move into the home-buyer's market, which in turn affects the number of tenants available to rent property. However, you cannot simply assume that all tenants are potential first home buyers. If we look at the "human factor" behind people renting, you will understand why tenants are not likely to be a dwindling commodity in the future. But before we do, let me ask you a simple question:

Have you ever rented?

Maybe you moved interstate and decided to rent for a few years until you got to know the area, or possibly you rented when you first left the family home, or perhaps you rented while you built your dream home, or maybe you holidayed in a unit on the coast. When I ask this question of those attending my seminars, I invariably get a show of hands of at least 95% of the audience.

Sadly, many people think of tenants as second-class citizens who don't have two brass razoos to rub together. The fact is that most tenants are just like you and me — normal, average, good living citizens — who rent for short periods of their lives for reasons other than those relating to finance. The graph below shows the reasons why people choose to rent.

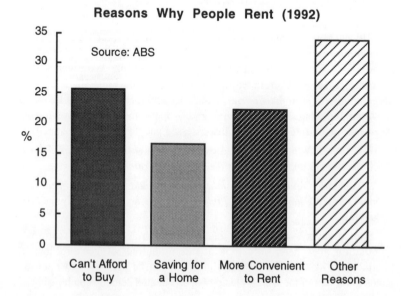

Contrary to what many people believe, most people rent for reasons other than that they can't afford to buy their own home. In fact, only 26% of all tenants could not afford to purchase a home, and the remaining 74% rented for the same sorts of reasons that you and I have rented at some stage. Some are saving for a home, some find it more convenient to rent, while yet many have other reasons.

In referring to the reasons tenants gave for preferring to rent, the Australian Bureau of Statistics report, "Social Indicators 1992" concluded:

Their reasons for living in rental accommodation are therefore more likely to be related to their transitional status than to their financial status.

So changing economic circumstances are not likely to significantly affect the supply of tenants in the future. Moreover, our changing lifestyles are more likely to create an *increase* in the number of tenants in the future. We have become a very mobile society with people moving from city to city, or State to State much more frequently than in the past.

There is also a greater tendency for people to demand a better quality of lifestyle. So although there are indications that some people cannot afford to purchase their own home, many simply cannot afford to purchase the home they desire. A survey by *Choice* magazine in 1986 also found this to be the case, in that many people rented because it offered a better quality of home than they could afford to purchase.

In other words, many young couples would rather pay $14,000 per year to rent a luxury residence, than pay $14,000 per year towards the loan repayments on a property of half the value, and half the quality. In the short term, there are definite social and economic benefits in renting. However, the future holds little hope for tenants who favour short-term gratification in preference to long-term financial security.

Clearly, investors are fulfilling a community need by providing rental accommodation. However, with today's changing lifestyles, tenants are now demanding a much better quality of rental accommodation than they were prepared to put up with in years gone by. This fact was brought home to me when one of our new tenants told me that they had just moved out of a not-so-well-looked-after house, in favour of moving into our very attractive, well maintained, landscaped property.

And there are signs that the number of tenants is increasing. Over the last two decades, the percentage of people renting has increased to more than 30% of the population (up from 24% in 1978). In a recent article in the *Women's Weekly* (April, 1994), the ANZ bank also observed this changing attitude to renting and commented:

... researchers are forecasting that over the next few years, the ratio of people renting may increase.

Too Many Property Investors?

Many property investors fear that too many people will jump on the band wagon and buy residential investment property in the future. This, they surmise, would increase the number of rental properties available, increase the vacancy rate and decrease the returns to property investors.

But how do these fears originate? The answer again is the "human factor". Have you ever noticed that just as you decide to buy a computer, the newspapers appear to be saturated with advertisements for computers? Yet the week before when you weren't interested, you never noticed any advertisements for computers at all. Or what about the time you had a crook back? I'll bet that before you hurt your back you never knew anyone with that problem, but suddenly you became aware that every other person either has a crook back or knows someone with one. It's one of those odd facts of life that as soon as you become interested in something you begin to see and hear about it everywhere, and it seems as though the whole world is interested in the same thing as you at exactly the same time.

And likewise with property investment. People often tell me that they saw an advertisement for one of my seminars, just as they were thinking about buying an investment property. The truth is that I have been doing seminars in their particular area for many years — they just never noticed them being advertised before. Many people have also told me that they saw my previous book *Building Wealth through Investment Property* in a bookstore on the very day that they went to town to sign for a loan on an investment property. And yet they had been to the bookstore dozens of times in the past year and never noticed it.

It's funny how people become acutely aware of the advertisements, books, seminars, and anything else associated with investment property, only when they become interested in it themselves. And then they make the assumption that because they are aware of it, everyone must be doing it, when in fact, most people are not.

Why is it that not everyone will become a property investor in the future? The answer lies simply in human nature. Apart from those who choose not to invest at all, there are many people who want to invest in property but just can't get started. They attend all the seminars, they read all the books, they can answer all the questions, and they earnestly believe that property investment is best — but they just can't take that first step. There are also many people who get started but they don't stay as property investors for very long. They are the ones who are continually looking for greener grass, or who don't follow the golden rules of property investment. Let's look at the human face of property investors so that you will then understand why so many people never start, while others never stay.

Some People Never Start

In 1979 in his book *Riches from Real Estate,* Fred Johnson, made the following observation about why people don't invest in property:

The answer is human nature: apathy — inertia — laziness — lack of time — lack of confidence in one's own ability to make decisions. 90% of the world's wealth is in the hands of 10% of the people — those 10% being the ones who overcome inertia or lack of confidence and go and do something about it. Of those who read this book, no more than 10% will take some positive step towards real estate profits after today. Not even 10% who are convinced will embark on some more profitable course of real estate investment in the future. That's just the nature of people and the reason why everybody isn't doing it.

Fred Johnson was not far from the truth when he observed that only 10% of people would become involved in investment property. The fact is that although most people believe that investing in property is the best of all (MLC Survey, *Courier Mail*, March 28, 1994), less than 10% actually do. The ABS in 1994 found that only 6% of adults invest in real estate, while a *Time* Morgan Poll (April, 1994) showed it to be just 7%. Even more interesting, the same *Time* survey found that this percentage had *not* changed since 1991 — a period in which interest rates fell dramatically and there had been wide publicity about negatively geared investment property.

Why do so few people invest in property? I could add thousands of reasons to Fred Johnson's list, but it would fill another book. Some of the reasons given to me over the years are:

We're just waiting until our son finishes high school and then we'll have enough money left over to invest in property.

I'm doing a lot of overtime at the moment and I'm just waiting to see if it lasts before we start. (He had been doing overtime for 20 years.)

There's too many people into property at the moment. We'll wait for the right time when there's not so many doing it.

Interest rates look like they're on the way up. We're just waiting to see if they stabilise before we start investing in property.

We've been looking for a good investment property for a while now. We're just waiting for the agent to let us know when he finds the right one. (These people went to their first seminar four years ago.)

My wife's father doesn't think it's a good idea to borrow money. (Incidentally, the wife's father was on the pension.)

My wife is going back to work next year. Then we'll have a few extra dollars to put into property. (He was earning $65,000 per year.)

But perhaps one of the most common reasons why people never start to invest in property, even though they *want* to, and even though they *realise* that they need to invest for their future, and even though they *acknowledge* that property is the way to go, is "I'm afraid to borrow money".

Fear! It stops us in our tracks. It prevents action when we know we should act. And yet most of our fears are completely unfounded. They are based on illogical perceptions of what "might" happen. Most people have a dread fear of sharks. They are afraid to go out in the water further than anyone else, are nervous about dangling their toes over the side of a boat, and suffer a panic attack if they fall off a boogie board in deep water.

These same people willingly get into a car and drive it around town, or up the coast for a holiday, or a thousand kilometres for a wedding, without any fear of a car accident whatsoever. But their fear of sharks and lack of fear of a car accident are way out of whack with reality.

According to the Australian Bureau of Statistics, on average, only *one* death per year has been caused by shark attack in Australia in the last two hundred years, while *2,000* people are killed on our roads in car accidents every year. What should we be more fearful of — sharks or cars?

Most people fear debt just as they fear sharks. Perhaps some statistics will help you to put debt in perspective. In the past five years, of the 2,000 loans arranged by one finance corporation for people to purchase an investment property, only one — just one — "fell over". And I was told that the particular person involved had failed to disclose a loan he had on a sports car. Compare this to the fact that in the past five years in Australia, almost 80% of people retired on an average income of $8,000 per year!

Again, I ask the question. What should we be more fearful of? A debt that can lead us to an early, wealthy retirement? Or getting to age 65 and finding that there is no age pension at all and you have done nothing about investing for the future? The fear of borrowing money *can* be overcome. It's simply a case of learning to be comfortable with debt, covering yourself for *all* possible eventualities, and understanding that debt, or gearing, is just a lever that you can use to allow you to retire early and wealthy. The fact is that it is almost impossible to become wealthy and retire early, unless you borrow money.

Another common reason why people never get started in investment property is "I can't afford to". Remember the gentleman who was waiting for his wife to go back to work so that they could afford to get started? The truth is that their poor spending habits are so entrenched that they will *never* be able to afford to buy an investment property. No matter how much some people earn, they just never have enough money. They are always waiting for the day when they will earn just that little bit extra.

I have known many people who have inherited several hundred thousand dollars, and who, a year later, were wishing that they had just a few extra hundred dollars to spare. Income makes little difference to your ability to buy property. I have said it before and I'll say it again — it's *what you do* with *what you earn* that counts. But the reality is that most people who *think* they can't afford to buy property, spend their money on "living for today". They are the "better buyers" who think along the lines of:

We're going to a New Year's Eve fancy dress party
— better buy a new pair of fancy shoes.   Cost: $80

I'm taking our new baby to show Grandma tomorrow
— better buy a new outfit for both baby and me.   Cost: $150

We've got friends staying with us for a few weeks
— better buy some new towels.   Cost: $40

I've just joined the tennis club
— better buy a new tracksuit.   Cost: $100

I can't be bothered cooking tonight
— better buy a take-away.   Cost $25

I've just found some bargain priced T-shirts for the kids
— better buy them three each.   Cost: $30

I've just seen a new thingummyjig on TV
— better buy one, or maybe two because it's cheaper.   Cost $39

We're a bit late with the shopping today
— better buy the kids some donuts and milkshakes for lunch. Cost: $10

I'll give up smoking next week
— better buy one more pack of cigarettes to last me 'til then.   Cost: $6

We're going on holidays at Christmas
— better buy the kids a new boogie board each.   Cost: $150

You probably think I'm talking about trivial items. How could a few dollars here and there possibly make any difference? Benjamin Franklin knew how these little things all counted when he said:

Beware of little expenses: a small leak will sink a great ship.

Obviously, the odd milkshake here and there won't break the piggy bank, nor will buying a new pair of shoes once in a while send you bankrupt, and it's nice to buy a new outfit for a new baby or some boogie boards for the kids at Christmas. But this kind of thinking ALL the time, every minute of the day, sinks any budget.

How many thousands of dollars have you let slip through your fingers on the little things in life that give you pleasure for just a few fleeting moments? My twelve year old son was quick to work out that people who smoke cigarettes "burn" more than $100,000 in a lifetime. How much do you spend on one-minute wonders? But it's when you extend this thinking to even larger items that you have a real problem.

I'm tired of watching football on a small TV
— better get a personal loan and buy a large-screened TV.   Cost: $3,000

Our best friends are staying with us for a few weeks
— better get a new lounge on hire purchase.   Cost: $5,000

It would be nice for the kids to see Disneyland
— better have a holiday in the USA on our credit cards.   Cost: $9,000

The kitchen is beginning to look a bit shabby
— better extend the house mortgage and buy a new one.   Cost: $10,000

Hubby would like a bigger boat
— better take out a home equity loan to buy bigger one.   Cost: $15,000

The kids love swimming at Christmas
— better talk to the bank about a swimming pool.   Cost: $20,000

Wouldn't it be great to go to Kakadu next month
— better see about finance for a new four wheel drive.   Cost: $35,000

All of the above comments were made by people in the prime of their working life, who now wonder why they have nothing substantial to show for their twenty years of work. These are the people who believe that they cannot afford to buy investment property, so they fritter away their dollars on consumables. The table below reveals what it would cost to buy each of the above items with a personal loan (at 14% interest over 5 years).

Are You Paying Off One of These Consumables?

Consumables Bought with Borrowed Funds	Original Value	Cost per Week
Large Flat Screen TV	$3,000	$16
Leather Lounge	$5,000	$27
Disneyland Holiday	$9,000	$47
Kitchen Cupboards and Appliances	$10,000	$54
New Boat	$15,000	$80
Swimming Pool and Bar BQ area	$20,000	$107
New Four Wheel Drive Car	$35,000	$187

And the trouble is that most people don't stop at just one of these items. As soon as they have finished paying off the car, they think they need a new "you beaut" TV, and as soon as they have paid off the TV, they think they need a new kitchen, and as soon as they have paid off the kitchen, they think they need a swimming pool, and as soon as they have finished paying off the pool it's time for a new car, and so it goes on.

Most people live for today believing that they cannot afford to buy investment property. They cannot understand, or prefer not to understand, that investment property can cost so little, because it might interfere with their priorities in life. I have heard many a person say that the real estate salesman is "pulling their leg" when he tells them how little it really costs to buy rental property. However, the table below (prepared for an investor on $45,000 per year) shows how little it can cost to borrow to buy an investment property.

The Small Cost of Buying an Investment Property

Investment Property Bought with Borrowed Funds	Original Value	Cost per Week
Small Two-Bedroom Unit	$100,000	$16
Small Two-Bedroom House	$120,000	$27
Average Three-Bedroom House	$140,000	$47
Large Two-Bedroom Townhouse	$150,000	$54
Large Three-Bedroom Townhouse	$160,000	$80
Two Average Three-Bedroom Houses	$280,000	$107
Three Average Three-Bedroom Houses	$420,000	$187

This table is not intended to be a guide to the actual cost of a particular property. The aim is to show you that the cost of borrowing to buy a rental property can be no more than the weekly cost of a leather lounge (a new lounge costs $27, which is the same cost as a small two-bedroom house) or a new boat ($80 is the same cost as a large three-bedroom townhouse). Even if you have paid off the boat, or whatever, after five years, it is probably worth much less than what you paid for it, while the equity you would have if you had borrowed to buy an investment property would put you well on your way to an early retirement.

Now don't get me wrong. There's nothing wrong with cheap T-shirts, gadgets, boats and new cars — but at some stage you need to set yourself some priorities. You *can* have your cake and eat it too, but not *all* of it. Save some for later — it will taste even better and you'll enjoy it more.

Some People Never Stay

For those people who do get started and do buy investment property, sadly, many just never stay. Many of them buy an investment property for all the wrong reasons and eventually sell up and move on to something else. Others do not get past their first property, while some just don't follow the golden rules and are forced to sell.

For many people, the decision to buy an investment property is not based on some logical decision to invest, but is more often based on the lemming reaction of following everyone else into the market. Now I'm not one for picking the right time to invest in property, but there are a few months at the peak of a cycle when it may be best to steer clear because of the frenzied buying spree created by the lemming reaction. One of the most interesting graphs I have put together is the one shown below. It is a combination of interest rates, median-priced residential property values in Sydney (although any city shows the same results), and the number of loans approved during the latter half of the eighties.

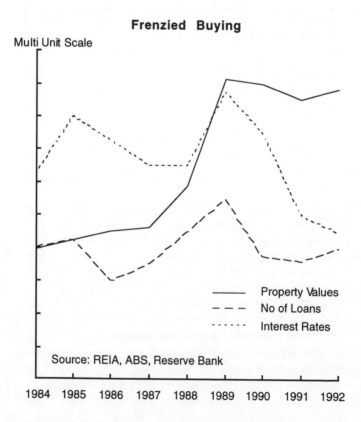

Frenzied Buying

Multi Unit Scale

— Property Values
- - - No of Loans
· · · · · · Interest Rates

Source: REIA, ABS, Reserve Bank

1984   1985   1986   1987   1988   1989   1990   1991   1992

This graph clearly shows that people got caught up in the buying frenzy of 1988/89 and borrowed to buy property when property values had peaked and interest rates were at their highest! Time and time again we see evidence that many people cannot make a decision totally independently of others. This lemming-like behaviour is a sure fire indicator that not all of these property investors will be stayers, and that some will fall by the wayside.

Would you like to know just how many property investors are stayers? In 1993, the Australian Bureau of Statistics found that in the previous five years, more than 30% of property investors had sold at least one residential property, while yet another 20% intended selling in the next two years. The reasons given for selling were:

Reasons for Selling Within Last 5 Years

Reasons intending to sell	% of Investors
Needed funds for family or business	20.4%
To invest in share market	0.8%
Inadequate return on investment	9.2%
To finance purchase elsewhere	30.5%
To realise capital gain	6.9%
Couldn't afford to keep it	9.8%
Divorce / separation	4.1%
Other	18.3%

Source: ABS

Obviously, many people (20.4%) needed funds for those unforeseen events that occur in either business or family. (Incidentally, you can't cash in your normal superannuation simply because your business needs it.) There were a small number of investors (9.2%) who "perceived" that they were receiving an inadequate return on their investment. (I would like the chance to prove to them otherwise.) A large number of investors (more than 30%) were into the "sell and buy again" mode, and then there were those investors (6.9%) who just wanted to see how much they had made.

Furthermore, of those who sold their investment property, almost 80% had sold their *only* investment property and were now no longer property investors. So you can see that many property investors are not property investors for very long and do not understand the principle of "buy and keep".

For those investors who do keep their first investment property, very few go on to buy more and this is shown in the following table.

Number of Properties Owned by Investors

Number of Residential Investment Properties Owned	% of People Owning Investment Property
1	4.7%
2	.8%
3	.2%
4	.1%
5 or more	.2%
TOTAL	**6.0%**

Source: ABS

Of the total of 6% of adult Australians who own a second property, just 4.7% own one; only .8% own two, while less than .5% own three or more properties — the minimum number I consider necessary to provide for a comfortable retirement. Obviously, long term investment in property is a commitment requiring financial discipline, something that many investors don't have. Lack of commitment and discipline are two of the reasons why most people fail at anything they attempt, whether it be for their wealth or for their health. I have already pointed out in Chapter 2 that only 7.7% of people retire on more than $20,000 per year. Noel Whittaker, in his best-selling book *Making Money Made Simple* also points out that less than 8% of people are successful financially. Rosemary Stanton in her book *The Diet Dilemma* suggests that only 1% of people succeed in dieting. And KRS Edstrom in *Healthy, Wealthy, and Wise* said of people on diets:

According to the Washington Post, only 1 in 200 will keep the weight off for more than five years.

No matter what aspect of life we refer to, or what way we look at it, less than 10% of people seem to be successful. The fact is that most people lack the self discipline to make diets work. And for exactly the same reasons, most people lack the commitment and discipline necessary to maintain a recipe for building wealth through investment property. What about you? Are you ready and willing to follow a plan to take responsibility for your own retirement? Or will you be one of those people who either never get started or never stay committed. If I can leave you with one thought:

If it is to be it's up to me.

Appendix
What If .....

Earlier in this book I answered many of the "what ifs" that property investors have been asking as a result of changing times. Some of the "what ifs" that were analysed were — the effect of varying inflation levels and changing personal tax rates on property investment. But these are just a few of the thousands of "what ifs" that property investors would like to know in order to satisfy themselves about investing in property.

The ones who don't take the time to understand are the ones who worry the most. They hear that vacancy rates are high and immediately think that the loss of a few weeks' rent will wipe them out. They discover that, in hindsight, they have paid too much for a property and immediately want to cut their losses and sell. And they question the effect of taking an interest-only loan instead of a principal and interest loan. If only these property investors would take the time to analyse and understand the real impact of "what ifs", they would realise that the loss of rent for a few weeks through vacancies is not a total disaster, and neither is having paid too much for an investment property if it is a median-priced residential property.

The only way to correctly answer "what ifs" is to take into account every financial detail and work out the rate of return on the investment in a particular circumstance. A computer makes such calculations easy. But if you have to call in your young children every time you want to use the video — take heart — computers and their software of today are easy to operate. The program we have devised will help you answer all your own "what ifs" about investment property, in a very user-friendly way.

In the following pages, I will look at many of the more common "what ifs" and I will explain the impact, or lack of impact, as simply as I can. In doing so, I have used the example $140,000 property (described on page 94) as a base for comparison, and the spreadsheet for this property is on the next page, with a detailed description in the following pages. Using this spreadsheet as a base, one or more of the variables were changed using the computer program to illustrate the overall impact of such changes on property as an investment.

The Basic Spreadsheet

Assumptions		Projected results over	5 yrs	10 yrs
Property value	$140,000	Property value	$200,988	$288,545
Deposit	$0	Equity	$54,988	$142,545
Rent per week	$180	After-tax return /yr	67.57%	36.45%
Cap. growth rate	7.50%	IF SOLD		
Inflation rate	5.00%	Selling costs & CGT	$11,241	$30,827
Interest rate	10.00%	Equity	$43,747	$111,718
Marginal tax rate	44.40%	After-tax return /yr	58.42%	32.14%

COMPUTER PROJECTIONS OVER 10 YEARS

ASSUMPTIONS	Inputs	1yr	2yr	3yr	5yr	10yr
Property value	140,000	150,500	161,788	173,922	200,988	288,545
Purchase costs	4,000					
Deposit	0					
Loan	146,000	146,000	146,000	146,000	146,000	146,000
Equity	-6,000	4,500	15,788	27,922	54,988	142,545
Capital growth	7.50%	7.50%	7.50%	7.50%	7.50%	7.50%
Inflation rate	5.00%	5.00%	5.00%	5.00%	5.00%	5.00%
GROSS RENT /wk,/yr	180	9,360	9,828	10,319	11,377	14,520
CASH DEDUCTIONS						
Loan interest I/O	10.00%	14,600	14,600	14,600	14,600	14,600
Property expenses	25.00%	2,340	2,457	2,580	2,844	3,630
PRE-TAX CASH FLOW	0	-7,580	-7,229	-6,860	-6,067	-3,710
NON-CASH DEDUCTIONS						
Deprec.-building	2.50%	2,000	2,000	2,000	2,000	2,000
Deprec.-fittings	10,300	2,800	1,875	1,406	791	188
Borrowing costs	2,000	400	400	400	400	
TOTAL DEDUCTIONS	0	22,140	21,332	20,986	20,635	20,418
TAX CREDIT (actual)	44.40%	5,154	4,905	4,736	4,299	2,854
AFTER-TAX CASH FLOW	0	-2,426	-2,324	-2,124	-1,768	-856
RATE OF RETURN -IRR	36.45%	———————	Your Cost Per Week		———————	
Before-tax return	65.57%	47	45	41	34	16

This spreadsheet is part of a report produced using the computer program
PIA (Property Investment Analysis) described on page 191 of this book.

Notes on Basic Spreadsheet

The figures in the column under the Inputs heading represent the variables used to calculate the projections over the following years. Although this particular analysis is over 10 years, the same process can be used to calculate the rate of return over any number of years. The notes that follow describe the variables. Each item is described in terms of the figures used in this particular example and alternative entries are suggested.

Property value

The $140,000 property value in this example represents the price paid for the property and is assumed to increase each year at a constant rate of compound growth. However, if renovations were carried out immediately after purchase, this could directly affect the property value and its potential for capital growth. Renovations may affect the property value, but not the stamp duty that is paid on the original purchase price. Also, if furniture is bought in addition to the property, the furniture costs will not necessarily add value to the property. However, they may increase the size of the loan, if you have borrowed to buy them, as well as increasing the depreciation claims.

Purchase costs

These include State Government stamp duty and your solicitor's fees. In this case, stamp duty is $3,650 (Qld rates for $140,000) and solicitor's fees are $350 (which may vary), giving total purchase costs of $4,000.

Deposit

The "deposit" represents the total amount of cash outlaid at the time of purchase. In this case, it is assumed that there is no cash deposit and that the total loan covers both the purchase price and all associated purchasing and borrowing costs. The size of the deposit that you may wish to make will affect the size of the loan and consequently your cash flow. Small deposits usually produce negative cash flows and large tax benefits — while large deposits usually produce positive cash flows and incur tax liabilities. The initial deposit is the first item in the after-tax cash flow.

Loan

This is the total of all costs (property price, purchase costs, loan costs, etc.) less the amount of the deposit. In this case, as the deposit is nil, the loan of $146,000 represents the total of all costs. If renovations were carried out immediately, or if the property was a holiday unit that required furniture, the loan may include these costs as well. The loan in this case is interest-only, and consequently, the debt remains constant for the entire 10 years. If a principal and interest loan was used, the debt would decrease with time until eventually the equity would be equal to the property value.

Equity

This is the difference between the property value and the loan. The equity increases in line with the increasing value of the property and, for a principal and interest loan, with decreasing debt. In the example, the loan was interest-only and so the equity of $142,545 after 10 years was solely due to the capital growth. Obviously, paying out the principal would increase the equity faster, but it would also decrease the rate of return, because you have to put in more of your own money, and you receive fewer tax benefits. Sales commission and capital gains tax have not been deducted here because the property is assumed to have been kept. However, it is possible to do a separate calculation taking these into account.

Capital growth

This is the expected long-term annual compound rate of growth in the value of the property (assumed to be 7.5% in the example). Although it is assumed to increase uniformly, the end result is not affected if the rate has varied over the time (yearly rates can be altered if desired). What is most important in the calculation is the end value of the property, not what has happened to the value along the way. As a result, the property may increase in value only in the final year, and the return would be the same as if growth was uniform.

Inflation rate

This is the expected long-term rate of inflation (assumed to be 5% per year in the example). Increases in rent and property expenses (insurance, rates, etc.) are assumed to increase uniformly at this rate, although the yearly rate can be altered if desired. If capital gains tax is to be considered, the inflation rate will also affect the actual taxable capital gain because the property value will be indexed to inflation.

Gross rent (/week and /year)

The first cell contains the expected weekly rent ($180 in this case), while the rest of the row represents the corresponding annual rent ($9,360 in the first year), which is calculated as 52 times the weekly rent. The annual rent is assumed to increase each year in line with inflation. In contrast to the application of capital growth to the property value, the regularity of increases in rent can affect the rate of return. This is because rents directly affect cash flows each and every year. Yet another consideration at this point is whether or not there are potential vacancies to be accounted for. These will affect the yearly rent projections.

Cash deductions

These differ from the "non-cash deductions" in that they are real cash outflows. Cash deductions consist of loan interest and rental expenses.

Loan interest

The first cell represents the interest rate, while the rest of the row represents the corresponding annual interest payments. In this example, the loan is assumed to be fixed-rate (10%) and interest-only, and so the interest payments are a constant $14,600 each year. However, with a principal and interest loan the interest component of the payment each year would decline, so that although the loan payment remains constant for the period of the loan, the tax benefits would be reduced over time. Also, with a principal and interest loan, the payment towards the principal would need to be accounted for separately, as it directly affects the cash flow and the equity, though not the tax refund.

Property expenses

These include the costs of rates, insurances and maintenance, etc., but exclude the interest on the loan. In the model, they account for 25% of the annual gross rent, which increases in line with inflation. The first year's expenses total $2,340, but these expenses might vary depending on the maintenance and whether or not you manage the property yourself.

Pre-tax cash flow

This is what flows in or out of your pocket before tax is taken into account. It is calculated as the gross rent less loan payments and property expenses. If you have an interest-only loan, as in the example, the loan payment equals the interest payment. But for a principal and interest loan, the loan payment is part principal payment and part interest payment and both must be taken into account.

Non-cash deductions

The three types of tax deductions that indirectly affect your cash flow in the form of tax benefits are "depreciation" on the building (more correctly called a capital allowance), depreciation on the fittings (such as carpets, curtains, etc.), and the loan or borrowing costs. They can significantly affect your after-tax cash flow and are often the forgotten items in property investment analysis. These do not affect the actual costs of expenses and loan payments, but they do affect the overall tax "loss" and consequently the tax benefits and after-tax cash flow.

"Depreciation" on building

This capital allowance is based on the initial construction cost of the building. In this example, the construction cost was $80,000, and the depreciation rate was 2.5% ($2,000) each year for 40 years. In other cases, the allowance may be nothing or 4% (over 25 years), depending on *when* the property was constructed. Although it adds tax benefits, it is not the sole criterion for choosing between a new or established property.

Depreciation on fittings

In this example, the cost of the fittings was assumed to be $10,300, consisting of items depreciated at varying rates. These rates can be self-assessed on the basis of the "life expectancy" of the item. In this case, the diminishing value method has been used instead of the prime cost method, because it confers tax benefits sooner and is thus more tax effective.

Borrowing costs

In the model, the costs are spread over 5 years. As a result, the tax benefits are reduced in the sixth year causing an increase in the after-tax cash flow in that year. It is possible for these borrowing costs to be written off over less than 5 years, depending on the term of the loan.

Total deductions

This is the sum of all deductions claimed — both cash and non-cash — and in the example amount to $22,140 in the first year. These deductions decline over the first few years, despite the fact that expenses rise with inflation. This is because the depreciation claims under the diminishing value method are initially high. After about eight years, the deductions increase in line with the additional expenses.

Tax credit

The first cell represents the marginal tax rate (44.40% in this example), and the rest of the row is the annual tax credit. There are two ways of calculating the tax credit. The easiest method is simply to assume that the entire loss (rent less deductions) occurs within the one marginal tax rate. This gives a reasonable approximation but a more precise method requires a knowledge of the exact taxable income. In this example, the precise method of using taxable income ($45,000 not shown) has been used. If a large deposit had been used on the property, then the property would more than likely produce a profit, in which case the items in this row would represent the tax liabilities.

After-tax cash flow

This is the amount of cash invested in, or gained from, the property in each year. In the model, the after-tax cash flow is negative in the initial stages (- $2,426 in the first year) and represents the investor's contribution. This should decrease with time as rents rise with inflation. Eventually a point would be reached where the rents overtake the loan payments and property expenses. At this time, there is a positive after-tax cash flow. It is possible to borrow the negative after-tax cash flows so that in effect, the property costs you nothing! I don't recommend this procedure, but it certainly presents an interesting mathematical concept. The after-tax cash flows are used to calculate the internal rate of return — IRR.

Rate of Return — IRR

This is the after-tax rate of return on all moneys invested in or gained from the property over the period considered. In the property investment example, the figures involved in the rate of return or IRR calculation are the after-tax cash flows each year, together with the equity after 10 years.

The Important Figures in the IRR Calculation

ASSUMPTIONS	Inputs	1yr	2yr	3yr	5yr	10yr
Equity	-6,000	4,500	15,788	27,922	54,988	142,545
AFTER-TAX CASH FLOW	0	-2,426	-2,324	-2,124	-1,768	-856

These after-tax cash flows represent your contribution to the property each year and could be regarded as similar to the deposits made into a bank account. If, after 10 years, there is $142,545 in equity, then the interest rate needed to produce this result would have had to have been 36.45% — which is the internal rate of return (IRR). There are many variations that can occur with these cash flows. For example, if there is a cash deposit, then this becomes the first item in the cash flow. And if the deposit is large enough, the subsequent annual after-tax cash flows become positive.

The rate of return on a negatively geared property will gradually decline with time. In this particular example, the IRR over 10 years is 36.45%, but if the same calculations were carried out over a 5 year period, the IRR would be 67.57%. The reasons for this are twofold. First, as rents rise with time, the tax benefits diminish to the point where tax must be paid. Secondly, the equity in the property increases with time, so the leverage effect on your initial outlay is reduced. Initially, the gearing ratio (the ratio of property value to equity) is $140,000 to 0, but after 10 years it is $288,545 to $142,545 (about 2:1), and after 20 years it is $594,700 to $448,700 — almost 1:1, which is virtually no gearing at all.

After a very long time (more than 25 years), the IRR would be reduced to around 15%, which is effectively the sum of the capital growth and net after-tax yield from the property. To maintain an overall higher rate of return, further properties should be bought as cash flow permits. This will regain the tax benefits and increase the overall gearing ratio, and enable your investment dollar to work harder.

Before-tax equivalent

This is the interest rate that your bank would have to pay if you were to get an equivalent rate of return. In this case, with a marginal rate of 44.40%, the rate over a 10 year period would have to be 65.57%.

What if the Vacancy Rate is High?

Many property investors believe that the loss of a few weeks' rent due to vacancies is a disaster. Personally, I believe that this situation could be avoided by keeping the property well maintained and by lowering the rent. I'd rather have 90% of something than 100% of nothing.

However, it is important for investors to understand that a higher than normal vacancy rate has very little effect on the overall returns from an investment property. Let's look at a situation where the vacancy rate is exceptionally high, at 20% each year for 10 years. This means that the property is vacant for about 10 weeks of the year, or that only 80% of the potential rent is received. A 20% vacancy rate is unheard of for residential property (though not uncommon for commercial property) and the current capital city vacancy rates range between 2% and 7% annually. So the situation I am about to describe is a worst-case scenario. The spreadsheet on the opposite page shows the overall picture.

In the first year, instead of receiving $9,360, the rent is only $7,488, or 80% of the potential rent. After taking all the cash flows into account, the property would cost only $70 per week — just $23 per week more than the $47 it would have cost for full occupancy. And the rate of return, which would now be 27.89%, is still a great return in anyone's language.

Why is the impact so small? The reason is that the tax man "pays" for almost half of your losses. The rent that you do not receive has the effect of lowering your total rental income so that there is a greater loss to be offset against personal income. This results in a higher tax refund ($5,817 instead of $5,154), which then lessens the burden of vacancies.

The table below gives the cost per week and the rate of return for a range of vacancy rates, so that you will understand just how little vacancies affect the overall returns. For a more normal situation of a 5% vacancy rate (about two to three weeks per year), the rate of return is barely affected at 33.96% and the extra cost per week is a mere $5 ($52 instead of $47).

Effect of Vacancies on Cost and Return

Vacancy Rate	0%	5%	10%	15%	20%
Cost Per Week	$47	$52	$58	$64	$70
Rate of Return	36.45%	33.96%	31.74%	29.72%	27.89%

Too many investors see only the dollars lost as a result of a few weeks' vacancy, when instead they should be looking at the overall cost and return from the investment. So it is important to put vacancies in perspective.

What if the Vacancy Rate is High?

Assumptions		Projected results over	5 yrs	10 yrs
Property value	$140,000	Property value	$200,988	$288,545
Deposit	$0	Equity	$54,988	$142,545
Rent per week	$180	After-tax return /yr	47.96%	27.89%
Cap. growth rate	7.50%	IF SOLD		
Inflation rate	5.00%	Selling costs & CGT	$11,241	$30,827
Interest rate	10.00%	Equity	$43,747	$111,718
Marginal tax rate	44.40%	After-tax return /yr	38.89%	23.53%

COMPUTER PROJECTIONS OVER 10 YEARS

ASSUMPTIONS	Inputs	1yr	2yr	3yr	5yr	10yr
Property value	140,000	150,500	161,788	173,922	200,988	288,545
Purchase costs	4,000					
Deposit	0					
Loan	146,000	146,000	146,000	146,000	146,000	146,000
Equity	-6,000	4,500	15,788	27,922	54,988	142,545
Capital growth	7.50%	7.50%	7.50%	7.50%	7.50%	7.50%
Inflation rate	5.00%	5.00%	5.00%	5.00%	5.00%	5.00%
GROSS RENT /wk,/yr	180	7,488	7,862	8,256	9,102	11,616
CASH DEDUCTIONS						
Loan interest I/O	10.00%	14,600	14,600	14,600	14,600	14,600
Property expenses	25.00%	2,340	2,457	2,580	2,844	3,630
PRE-TAX CASH FLOW	0	-9,452	-9,195	-8,924	-8,343	-6,614
NON-CASH DEDUCTIONS						
Deprec.-building	2.50%	2,000	2,000	2,000	2,000	2,000
Deprec.-fittings	10,300	2,800	1,875	1,406	791	188
Borrowing costs	2,000	400	400	400	400	
TOTAL DEDUCTIONS	0	22,140	21,332	20,986	20,635	20,418
TAX CREDIT (actual)	44.40%	5,817	5,601	5,552	5,309	4,260
AFTER-TAX CASH FLOW	0	-3,635	-3,594	-3,372	-3,034	-2,354
RATE OF RETURN -IRR	27.89%	——————— Your Cost Per Week ———————				
Before-tax return	50.17%	70	69	65	58	45

Variables Changed from Basic Spreadsheet on page 162

Vacancy Rate = 20% each year

What if I Buy a Holiday Unit?

A holiday unit can be just as good an investment as a permanently let property — provided it is treated as a business proposition, not a luxury second house for the family. In many instances, a holiday unit is bought as a combination "investment" plus "we'll get to use it too". However, most people want to use their unit at Christmas and Easter — two of the peak times for holiday letting — and then wonder why their investment doesn't perform. Another trap for these "pseudo" investors is that they let their friends and the friends of the friends and the relatives of the friends of the friends rent it at discounted rates. If you can afford to use your unit as a luxury, that's fine — at least it's better than borrowing to buy a luxury car. Otherwise think carefully about *why* you are buying a holiday unit.

Luxuries aside, if the unit is bought purely as a business proposition, then the figures stack up and the property should give returns that are just as good as a permanently rented property. Let's look at a few differences that occur when a holiday unit is treated strictly as an investment.

If you refer to the spreadsheet on the opposite page, you will see that the total annual rent is $12,200, made up of a variety of levels. A typical rental scenario for a holiday unit on the Sunshine Coast of Queensland is:

Peak season (Christmas holidays)　=　7　wks at $650/wk　=　$4,550

Shoulder season (mid-yr holidays)　=　4　wks at $350/wk　=　$1,400

Off season (40% vacancy)　=　25　wks at $250/wk　=　$6,250

Total rent　　　　　　　　　　　　　　　　**= $12,200**

The expenses at $6,100 (50% of the gross rent) are higher than for a permanent tenancy and include agent's fees (about 12% for holiday letting), maintenance (which must include cleaning costs after each occupancy), and body corporate fees (which might include lift costs), etc.

Holiday units also qualify for substantial depreciation allowances on both the furniture and the fittings, and in the model, with the total value of furniture and fittings being $25,000, the claim is $10,350 in the first year. This also includes a special one-off write-off for items such as linen and cutlery, which can now be depreciated at 100% if they are valued at less than $300. (The total value of such items in this case is $5,000.) Also, the common property such as the swimming pool, pool filters and lifts can be claimed pro-rata, based on lot entitlement.

Overall, this holiday unit would provide an after-tax return of 33.66%, which is not significantly different from the returns of the permanently let example property (36.45%). So if you are prepared to buy a holiday unit and use it yourself during the off season when it is *available* for renting but *not* rented, it can be just as good an investment as a permanent tenancy.

What if I Buy a Holiday Unit?

Assumptions		Projected results over	5 yrs	10 yrs
Property value	$140,000	Property value	$200,988	$288,545
Deposit	$0	Equity	$44,988	$132,545
Rent per week	$235	After-tax return /yr	63.23%	33.66%
Cap. growth rate	7.50%	IF SOLD		
Inflation rate	5.00%	Selling costs & CGT	$11,241	$30,827
Interest rate	10.00%	Equity	$33,747	$101,718
Marginal tax rate	44.40%	After-tax return /yr	49.54%	28.46%

COMPUTER PROJECTIONS OVER 10 YEARS

ASSUMPTIONS	Inputs	1yr	2yr	3yr	5yr	10yr
Property value	140,000	150,500	161,788	173,922	200,988	288,545
Purchase costs	4,000					
Deposit	0					
Loan	156,000	156,000	156,000	156,000	156,000	156,000
Equity	-16,000	-5,500	5,788	17,922	44,988	132,545
Capital growth	7.50%	7.50%	7.50%	7.50%	7.50%	7.50%
Inflation rate	5.00%	5.00%	5.00%	5.00%	5.00%	5.00%
GROSS RENT /wk,/yr	235	12,200	12,810	13,451	14,829	18,927
CASH DEDUCTIONS						
Loan interest I/O	10.00%	15,600	15,600	15,600	15,600	15,600
Property expenses	50.00%	6,100	6,405	6,725	7,415	9,463
PRE-TAX CASH FLOW	0	-9,500	-9,195	-8,874	-8,185	-6,137
NON-CASH DEDUCTIONS						
Deprec.-building	2.50%	2,000	2,000	2,000	2,000	2,000
Deprec.-fittings	25,000	10,350	3,883	2,826	1,511	336
Borrowing costs	2,000	400	400	400	400	
TOTAL DEDUCTIONS	0	34,450	28,288	27,551	26,926	27,399
TAX CREDIT (actual)	44.40%	8,506	6,311	6,037	5,559	4,101
AFTER-TAX CASH FLOW	0	-994	-2,884	-2,837	-2,626	-2,036
RATE OF RETURN -IRR	33.66%	————————	Your Cost Per Week	————————		
Before-tax return	60.54%	19	55	55	51	39

Variables Changed from Basic Spreadsheet on page 162:

Fittings = $25,000; Rent = Holiday Rates; Property Expenses = 50% of rent

What if I Buy a Property in Joint Names?

Investors must decide whether to purchase an investment property in joint or in single names. The decision is based on a number of factors. First, what are the income levels of the two partners? Second, is the property to be bought for cash or is it to be negatively geared? Third, is the property to be sold in a few years or to be kept for the long term? And fourth, on a personal note, does the ownership infringe on the rights of one person or the other (e.g. in a defacto relationship)?

If the property is bought for the short-term for cash and no loan, then it is best bought in the name of the lowest-income earner. This way the tax on the rent is minimised, and a future sale will incur minimal CGT on the profits. However, if the property is bought for the long term, with no cash deposit and full borrowings, then, personal considerations aside, it is best bought in the name of the highest-income earner. In this way the personal tax benefits are maximised through negative gearing.

The spreadsheet opposite is for a joint ownership (50-50 split) where one person earns $45,000 and the other $5,400. It shows the combined result for the two halves, the only differences from the basic spreadsheet being the tax refund and rate of return. Instead of a tax refund of $5,154 (for single ownership and income $45,000), the combined tax refund is just $2,837 and the return is 24.34%. The table below shows how this occurs.

Joint versus Single Ownership of Rental Property

TAX BENEFITS	Joint Names		Single Name
	Investor	Spouse	Investor
Present taxable income:	45,000	5,400	45,000
Rental income:	4,680	4,680	9,360
Total income:	49,680	10,080	54,360
Rental deductions:	11,070	11,070	22,140
New taxable income:	38,610	-990	32,220
Present tax:	12,582	0	12,582
New tax:	9,745	0	7,428
Tax saving:	2,837	0	5,154

If the property is bought in joint names, the rent and tax deductions are equally divided. The investor earning $45,000, receives only half the rent ($4,680) and half the deductions ($11,070), and hence the tax refund is $2,837. However, the partner earning $5,400 also receives half the rent and half the tax deductions, but with no present tax, there is no tax refund. In this situation, the negative gearing benefits have been lost and it would have been better to have bought the property in the single name only.

What if I Buy a Property in Joint Names?

Assumptions		Projected results over	5 yrs	10 yrs
Property value	$140,000	Property value	$200,988	$288,545
Deposit	$0	Equity	$54,988	$142,545
Rent per week	$180	After-tax return /yr	37.24%	24.34%
Cap. growth rate	7.50%	IF SOLD		
Inflation rate	5.00%	Selling costs & CGT	$9,075	$24,454
Interest rate	10.00%	Equity	$45,913	$118,090
Marginal tax rate	44.40%	After-tax return /yr	30.36%	21.11%

COMPUTER PROJECTIONS OVER 10 YEARS

ASSUMPTIONS	Inputs	1yr	2yr	3yr	5yr	10yr
Property value	140,000	150,500	161,788	173,922	200,988	288,545
Purchase costs	4,000					
Deposit	0					
Loan	146,000	146,000	146,000	146,000	146,000	146,000
Equity	-6,000	4,500	15,788	27,922	54,988	142,545
Capital growth	7.50%	7.50%	7.50%	7.50%	7.50%	7.50%
Inflation rate	5.00%	5.00%	5.00%	5.00%	5.00%	5.00%
GROSS RENT /wk,/yr	180	9,360	9,828	10,319	11,377	14,520
CASH DEDUCTIONS						
Loan interest I/O	10.00%	14,600	14,600	14,600	14,600	14,600
Property expenses	25.00%	2,340	2,457	2,580	2,844	3,630
PRE-TAX CASH FLOW	0	-7,580	-7,229	-6,860	-6,067	-3,710
NON-CASH DEDUCTIONS						
Deprec.-building	2.50%	2,000	2,000	2,000	2,000	2,000
Deprec.-fittings	10,300	2,800	1,875	1,406	791	188
Borrowing costs	2,000	400	400	400	400	
TOTAL DEDUCTIONS	0	22,140	21,332	20,986	20,635	20,418
TAX CREDIT (joint)	44.40%	2,837	2,608	2,479	2,473	2,017
AFTER-TAX CASH FLOW	0	-4,743	-4,621	-4,381	-3,594	-1,693
RATE OF RETURN -IRR	24.34%	———————	Your Cost	Per Week	———————	
Before-tax return	43.78%	91	89	84	69	33

Variables Changed from Basic Spreadsheet on page 162:

Joint Names; Investor's Income = $45,000; Spouse's Income = $5,400

What if I Have to Pay Land Tax?

With many investors, land tax is seen as a huge burden that adversely affects property investment to such an extent that it is no longer a viable proposition. However, as you will see, these fears are unfounded.

Although land tax is inevitable for the property investor committed to increasing their portfolio of properties, the effect on the overall returns is negligible. Land tax is a State-levied tax, and can vary greatly from State to State and Governments have always viewed it as a revenue collecting exercise from those who can seemingly afford to pay.

For most people who own just their principal place of residence, the tax does not apply. It is only levied on those who have several properties (in the one State) over and above their own home. Let's do an example so that you can see just how little land tax affects property investment.

Consider the situation where land tax of $2,400 has just been levied on an investor as a result of purchasing a fourth investment property for a cost of $140,000. Although this tax applies with the purchase of the fourth property, the tax is levied as a result of owning the first three investment properties as well, and in analysing returns, it should therefore be spread over all four. (In a normal tax return, land tax usually is accounted for in a "general section", rather than the individual property.) Consequently, the investor effectively pays land tax of $600 for each of their four investment properties.

If you refer to the spreadsheet on the opposite page, you can see the effect of paying land tax of $600 per property in the first year, increasing in line with inflation over the ensuing years. The expenses have now increased to $2,940 (up $600 from $2,340) and as a result, the total tax deductions have increased $600 to $22,740. The tax refund is then $213 higher, at $5,367 instead of $5,154. This increase compensates for more than one third of the land tax and it is this tax benefit that lessens the impact of land tax on property investment.

The bottom line is that for each property, land tax costs the investor just seven dollars a week extra ($54 up from $47) and has almost no effect on the overall returns. In this scenario, the rate of return has changed very little from 36.45% to 33.31% per annum compound.

Yes, Governments can increase land tax at random as a source of funds. And for very low income earners with very large land holdings (such as pensioners with several large blocks of non-income producing land), land tax can have a significant effect. However, for negatively geared property investors with holdings of many median-priced residential properties, the effect of paying land tax is negligible.

What if I Have to Pay Land Tax?

Assumptions		Projected results over	5 yrs	10 yrs
Property value	$140,000	Property value	$200,988	$288,545
Deposit	$0	Equity	$54,988	$142,545
Rent per week	$180	After-tax return /yr	60.30%	33.31%
Cap. growth rate	7.50%	IF SOLD		
Inflation rate	5.00%	Selling costs & CGT	$11,241	$30,827
Interest rate	10.00%	Equity	$43,747	$111,718
Marginal tax rate	44.40%	After-tax return /yr	51.18%	28.98%

COMPUTER PROJECTIONS OVER 10 YEARS

ASSUMPTIONS	Inputs	1yr	2yr	3yr	5yr	10yr
Property value	140,000	150,500	161,788	173,922	200,988	288,545
Purchase costs	4,000					
Deposit	0					
Loan	146,000	146,000	146,000	146,000	146,000	146,000
Equity	-6,000	4,500	15,788	27,922	54,988	142,545
Capital growth	7.50%	7.50%	7.50%	7.50%	7.50%	7.50%
Inflation rate	5.00%	5.00%	5.00%	5.00%	5.00%	5.00%
GROSS RENT /wk,/yr	180	9,360	9,828	10,319	11,377	14,520
CASH DEDUCTIONS						
Loan interest I/O	10.00%	14,600	14,600	14,600	14,600	14,600
Property expenses	31.41%	2,940	3,087	3,241	3,574	4,561
PRE-TAX CASH FLOW	0	-8,180	-7,859	-7,522	-6,796	-4,640
NON-CASH DEDUCTIONS						
Deprec.-building	2.50%	2,000	2,000	2,000	2,000	2,000
Deprec.-fittings	10,300	2,800	1,875	1,406	791	188
Borrowing costs	2,000	400	400	400	400	
TOTAL DEDUCTIONS	0	22,740	21,962	21,648	21,365	21,349
TAX CREDIT (actual)	44.40%	5,367	5,128	5,030	4,623	3,305
AFTER-TAX CASH FLOW	0	-2,813	-2,731	-2,492	-2,173	-1,335
RATE OF RETURN -IRR	33.31%	———————	Your Cost	Per Week	———————	
Before-tax return	59.92%	54	53	48	42	26

Variables Changed from Basic Spreadsheet on page 162:

Land Tax = $600

What if I Have to Pay Mortgage Insurance?

Many people are attracted to a particular financial institution because of the low interest rates and then find, to their disgust and dismay, that they must pay more than one thousand dollars in mortgage insurance. For example. Suppose an investor is using a block of land valued at $60,000 to help secure a loan for the purchase of our example $140,000 property. The loan to value ratio (LV ratio) would then be as follows:

Total loan (including costs)   = $146,000

Total value of properties mortgaged   = $200,000 ($140,000 + $60,000)

Loan to value ratio   =   Total Loan

Total Property Value

= $146,000

$200,000

=   73%

Now let's suppose that this particular financial institution will only lend to an LV ratio of 70% without mortgage insurance and asks the investor for additional security (either another house or another block of land he owns) or else he must pay mortgage insurance of $3,000. (I have chosen an exceptionally high value for mortgage insurance to show you how even absurd amounts have little affect on the returns from property.)

At this point, most investors have a mini heart attack and either start looking around for another financial institution that does not charge mortgage insurance (but where the interest rate is probably higher) or relent and offer additional security to reduce the LV ratio to below 70%. Personally, I would prefer to pay the $3,000, instead of either accepting an interest rate of 11% from another institution where I would pay no mortgage insurance or putting up another property as security. Why?

The spreadsheet on the opposite page shows the effect of adding an additional $3,000 mortgage insurance charge to the borrowing costs, which would then take the total borrowing costs to $5,000. Over 10 years, the returns from the property would be 36.21% instead of the normal 36.45% — an insignificant difference — and the cost per week in the first year drops by just $1 to $46. How can this be so?

First, the cost of the mortgage insurance can be borrowed, and hence the extra interest (up $300) on the extra loan (up $3,000) is tax deductible. And secondly, because the borrowing costs are written off over five years ($1,000 claimed each year), the mortgage insurance itself is tax deductible. To me, paying mortgage insurance and giving the bank the *least* amount of collateral to secure a loan is a far more flexible option.

What if I Have to Pay Mortgage Insurance?

Assumptions		Projected results over	5 yrs	10 yrs
Property value	$140,000	Property value	$200,988	$288,545
Deposit	$0	Equity	$51,988	$139,545
Rent per week	$180	After-tax return /yr	65.88%	36.21%
Cap. growth rate	7.50%	IF SOLD		
Inflation rate	5.00%	Selling costs & CGT	$11,241	$30,827
Interest rate	10.00%	Equity	$40,747	$108,718
Marginal tax rate	44.40%	After-tax return /yr	56.12%	31.75%

COMPUTER PROJECTIONS OVER 10 YEARS

ASSUMPTIONS	Inputs	1yr	2yr	3yr	5yr	10yr
Property value	140,000	150,500	161,788	173,922	200,988	288,545
Purchase costs	4,000					
Deposit	0					
Loan	149,000	149,000	149,000	149,000	149,000	149,000
Equity	-9,000	1,500	12,788	24,922	51,988	139,545
Capital growth	7.50%	7.50%	7.50%	7.50%	7.50%	7.50%
Inflation rate	5.00%	5.00%	5.00%	5.00%	5.00%	5.00%
GROSS RENT /wk,/yr	180	9,360	9,828	10,319	11,377	14,520
CASH DEDUCTIONS						
Loan interest I/O	10.00%	14,900	14,900	14,900	14,900	14,900
Property expenses	25.00%	2,340	2,457	2,580	2,844	3,630
PRE-TAX CASH FLOW	0	-7,880	-7,529	-7,160	-6,367	-4,010
NON-CASH DEDUCTIONS						
Deprec.-building	2.50%	2,000	2,000	2,000	2,000	2,000
Deprec.-fittings	10,300	2,800	1,875	1,406	791	188
Borrowing costs	5,000	1,000	1,000	1,000	1,000	
TOTAL DEDUCTIONS	0	23,040	22,232	21,886	21,535	20,718
TAX CREDIT (actual)	44.40%	5,473	5,224	5,136	4,698	3,000
AFTER-TAX CASH FLOW	0	-2,407	-2,305	-2,024	-1,669	-1,010
RATE OF RETURN -IRR	36.21%	———— Your Cost Per Week ————				
Before-tax return	65.12%	46	44	39	32	19

Variables Changed from Basic Spreadsheet on page 162:

Mortgage Insurance = $3,000 (total borrowing costs = $5,000)

What if I Pay Too Much for the Property?

Many investors continually hunt for that elusive bargain, expecting that they will be making a killing on property overnight. It is only human nature for most people to get a warm and fuzzy feeling if they think they have done well for themselves, and have paid less for the property than they perceived it was worth. For short-term property traders, where it is essential to make a profit on the property in a very short period of time, negotiating a bargain price is very important. However, for long-term property investors, negotiating a rock bottom price is not critical to the success of the investment.

But many investors are not adept at using the negotiating tool, and so wrongly believe that they must spend months waiting and searching for the perfect bargain. Apart from the fact that I believe that these "bargains" turn up every other week, I also believe that it is not necessary to wait for that cheap bargain to pop up. This doesn't mean that you must accept the vendor's price for a property. It is important to distinguish between the asking price and the market value, as the two may or may not be the same. You won't know the real value until you've done enough homework.

However, some investors find themselves in quite the reverse situation. Rather than having bought a bargain, they find that, in hindsight, they have paid too much for the property. Usually, the investor's first reaction is to feel devastated or cheated, or both. But let's look at how forgiving a mistake of this kind would be in the long term for median-priced property.

Suppose that an investor buys a property for $140,000 but then later discovers that the property was worth only $130,000. The spreadsheet opposite shows this situation, where the loan for the property is still the same at $146,000, but the property value starts at $130,000.

If the investor had been a trader and had sold the property after only two years, he would lose, as there is no equity in the second year (it is minus $6,250). However, it is a completely different story for an investor keeping the property for the long term (which he should be doing anyway). The bottom line is that the after-tax return of 33.68% on the investment has not changed significantly from the return of 36.45% that would have been received had the property been truly worth the paid price of $140,000.

It seems extraordinary that an apparent loss of $10,000 means very little in the long term. Why is this so? The blow is softened by the fact that the interest on the additional amount of $10,000 is tax deductible, so in effect the tax man is paying for part of the "mistake". As you can see, paying too much for a property has very little effect on the investor — provided the investment is median-priced residential property and is held for the long term.

What if I Pay Too Much for the Property?

Assumptions		Projected results over	5 yrs	10 yrs
Property value	$130,000	Property value	$186,632	$267,934
Deposit	$0	Equity	$40,632	$121,934
Rent per week	$180	After-tax return /yr	53.89%	33.68%
Cap. growth rate	7.50%	IF SOLD		
Inflation rate	5.00%	Selling costs & CGT	$10,294	$28,416
Interest rate	10.00%	Equity	$30,338	$93,518
Marginal tax rate	44.40%	After-tax return /yr	42.13%	29.02%

COMPUTER PROJECTIONS OVER 10 YEARS

ASSUMPTIONS	Inputs	1yr	2yr	3yr	5yr	10yr
Property value	130,000	139,750	150,231	161,499	186,632	267,934
Purchase costs	4,000					
Deposit	0					
Loan	146,000	146,000	146,000	146,000	146,000	146,000
Equity	-16,000	-6,250	4,231	15,499	40,632	121,934
Capital growth	7.50%	7.50%	7.50%	7.50%	7.50%	7.50%
Inflation rate	5.00%	5.00%	5.00%	5.00%	5.00%	5.00%
GROSS RENT /wk,/yr	180	9,360	9,828	10,319	11,377	14,520
CASH DEDUCTIONS						
Loan interest I/O	10.00%	14,600	14,600	14,600	14,600	14,600
Property expenses	25.00%	2,340	2,457	2,580	2,844	3,630
PRE-TAX CASH FLOW	0	-7,580	-7,229	-6,860	-6,067	-3,710
NON-CASH DEDUCTIONS						
Deprec.-building	2.50%	2,000	2,000	2,000	2,000	2,000
Deprec.-fittings	10,300	2,800	1,875	1,406	791	188
Borrowing costs	2,000	400	400	400	400	
TOTAL DEDUCTIONS	0	22,140	21,332	20,986	20,635	20,418
TAX CREDIT (actual)	44.40%	5,154	4,905	4,736	4,299	2,854
AFTER-TAX CASH FLOW	0	-2,426	-2,324	-2,124	-1,768	-856
RATE OF RETURN -IRR	33.68%	———	Your Cost Per Week			———
Before-tax return	60.58%	47	45	41	34	16

Variables Changed from Basic Spreadsheet on page 162:
Property Value = $130,000; Loan = $146,000

What if I'm -ve Geared with a +ve Cash Flow?

Property investors sometimes encounter a rather strange phenomenon called negative gearing with a positive cash flow. Let's first look at the more normal situation so that you will understand the difference.

Negatively Geared With a Negative Cash Flow

Negative Gearing

= Tax Deductions > Rent

= Tax Refund

Negative Cash Flow

= (Rental Expenses + Loan Payments) > (Rent + Tax Refund)

= Negative after-tax cash flow

In other words, in a normal negative gearing situation, the investor receives a tax refund but there is a negative after-tax cash flow because the rental expenses plus the loan payments are greater than the rent plus the tax refund. The more unusual situation would be this:

Negatively Geared with a Positive Cash Flow

Negative Gearing

= Tax Deductions > Rent

= Tax Refund

Positive Cash Flow

= (Rent + Tax Refund) > (Rental Expenses + Loan Payments)

= Positive after-tax cash flow

In this case the investor receives a tax refund because the tax deductions exceed the gross rent, but at the same time the after-tax cash flow is positive. How does this contradictory situation occur? It is brought about by the existence of non-cash deductions in combination with either high rent, low loan payments or low rental expenses. Let's look at an example.

The spreadsheet opposite is for the situation where non-cash deductions are initially $5,200 and the interest rate is low at 7%. In the first year, the tax refund is $3,604 but the overall cash flow is positive at $404 per year. In effect, this investor is making money out of nothing! In cases like this, it is a mathematical impossibility to calculate the rate of return and the IRR appears as "????". However, it would pay to ensure that the situation was not just a temporary aberration caused by short term changes (e.g. if the interest rate was extremely low but variable), which could lead to a substantial negative cash flow later when things returned to normal.

What if I'm -ve Geared with a +ve Cash Flow?

Assumptions		Projected results over	5 yrs	10 yrs
Property value	$140,000	Property value	$200,988	$288,545
Deposit	$0	Equity	$54,988	$142,545
Rent per week	$180	After-tax return /yr	?????	?????
Cap. growth rate	7.50%	IF SOLD		
Inflation rate	5.00%	Selling costs & CGT	$11,634	$30,827
Interest rate	7.00%	Equity	$43,354	$111,718
Marginal tax rate	44.40%	After-tax return /yr	?????	?????

COMPUTER PROJECTIONS OVER 10 YEARS

ASSUMPTIONS	Inputs	1yr	2yr	3yr	5yr	10yr
Property value	140,000	150,500	161,788	173,922	200,988	288,545
Purchase costs	4,000					
Deposit	0					
Loan	146,000	146,000	146,000	146,000	146,000	146,000
Equity	-6,000	4,500	15,788	27,922	54,988	142,545
Capital growth	7.50%	7.50%	7.50%	7.50%	7.50%	7.50%
Inflation rate	5.00%	5.00%	5.00%	5.00%	5.00%	5.00%
GROSS RENT /wk,/yr	180	9,360	9,828	10,319	11,377	14,520
CASH DEDUCTIONS						
Loan interest I/O	7.00%	10,220	10,220	10,220	10,220	10,220
Property expenses	25.00%	2,340	2,457	2,580	2,844	3,630
PRE-TAX CASH FLOW	0	-3,200	-2,849	-2,480	-1,687	670
NON-CASH DEDUCTIONS						
Deprec.-building	2.50%	2,000	2,000	2,000	2,000	2,000
Deprec.-fittings	10,300	2,800	1,875	1,406	791	188
Borrowing costs	2,000	400	400	400	400	
TOTAL DEDUCTIONS	0	17,760	16,952	16,606	16,255	16,038
TAX CREDIT (actual)	44.40%	3,604	3,163	2,791	2,354	735
AFTER-TAX CASH FLOW	0	404	314	311	667	1,405
RATE OF RETURN -IRR	?????	———————— Your Cost Per Week ————————				
Before-tax return	?????					

Variables Changed from Basic Spreadsheet on page 162:

Interest Rate = 7%

What if I Take a P & I Loan?

Many property investors take a principal and interest loan (P&I loan) instead of an interest-only loan because they feel much more comfortable reducing the debt. I consider that if you are investing in property you must be able to sleep at night, and taking a P&I loan may be better and cheaper than taking tranquillisers. However, personal factors aside, there are many financial advantages in taking an interest-only loan.

First, it is very difficult to fix the interest rate with a P&I loan, and this adds a degree of uncertainty. Secondly, the principal component is not tax deductible (only the interest) and therefore is paid from after-tax dollars earned elsewhere, making the real cost almost double. Thirdly, the extra principal payment towards just one property would work much harder if it were put towards more property where more capital is working for the same cost. And fourthly, the extra payment made towards the principal is an additional commitment — you *must* pay the extra or else!

Let's look at the spreadsheet opposite so that you can see how a P&I loan affects property investment. The loan considered in the spreadsheet is a P&I loan with a 15 year term. Only the interest component of the loan is tax deductible, and this is shown as part of the cash deductions, while the principal component is shown separately in the deposit row. These two separate components are shown in the table below with the sum of the two constituting the loan payment of $18,827.

Deposit/Principal	0	4,426	4,890	5,402	6,592	10,846
Loan interest P&I	10.00%	14,401	13,937	13,425	12,235	7,981
Loan Payment		18,827	18,827	18,827	18,827	18,827

The effect of taking a P&I loan is that the cost per week is increased from $47 per week in the first year for an interest-only loan, to $129 per week. The additional $82 per week would easily allow the purchase of a second property. And remember, this $82 comes from after-tax dollars, so it is necessary to earn almost $140 to receive $82 in income after tax. The rate of return is also affected and is reduced to 21.17%. This is still a good return, but it could be better at 36.45% with an interest-only loan.

For those who like the benefits of an interest-only loan, but who wish to see some of the principal paid off, a compromise would be to save the additional principal payment in a separate account (perhaps in the name of the lower income earner) and when the interest-only loan is refinanced after say five years, money could then be put towards reducing the loan. There is a big difference in commitment between *having* to pay the extra each week and *wanting* to pay it every few years.

What if I Take a P & I Loan?

Assumptions		Projected results over	5 yrs	10 yrs
Property value	$140,000	Property value	$200,988	$288,545
Deposit	$0	Equity	$82,266	$214,703
Rent per week	$180	After-tax return /yr	36.03%	21.17%
Cap. growth rate	7.50%	IF SOLD		
Inflation rate	5.00%	Selling costs & CGT	$11,241	$30,827
Interest rate	10.00%	Equity	$71,025	$183,876
Marginal tax rate	44.40%	After-tax return /yr	30.31%	18.20%

COMPUTER PROJECTIONS OVER 10 YEARS

ASSUMPTIONS	Inputs	1yr	2yr	3yr	5yr	10yr
Property value	140,000	150,500	161,788	173,922	200,988	288,545
Purchase costs	4,000					
Deposit/Principal	0	4,426	4,890	5,402	6,592	10,846
Loan	146,000	141,574	136,684	131,282	118,722	73,842
Equity	-6,000	8,926	25,104	42,640	82,266	214,703
Capital growth	7.50%	7.50%	7.50%	7.50%	7.50%	7.50%
Inflation rate	5.00%	5.00%	5.00%	5.00%	5.00%	5.00%
GROSS RENT /wk,/yr	180	9,360	9,828	10,319	11,377	14,520
CASH DEDUCTIONS						
Loan interest P&I	10.00%	14,401	13,937	13,425	12,235	7,981
Property expenses	25.00%	2,340	2,457	2,580	2,844	3,630
PRE-TAX CASH FLOW	0	-11,807	-11,456	-11,088	-10,294	-7,937
NON-CASH DEDUCTIONS						
Deprec.-building	2.50%	2,000	2,000	2,000	2,000	2,000
Deprec.-fittings	10,300	2,800	1,875	1,406	791	188
Borrowing costs	2,000	400	400	400	400	
TOTAL DEDUCTIONS	0	21,941	20,669	19,811	18,270	13,798
TAX CREDIT (actual)	44.40%	5,084	4,670	4,214	3,249	-349
AFTER-TAX CASH FLOW	0	-6,723	-6,786	-6,874	-7,045	-8,286
RATE OF RETURN -IRR	21.17%	————	Your Cost	Per Week	————	
Before-tax return	38.08%	129	131	132	135	159

Variables Changed from Basic Spreadsheet on page 162:

Loan Type = principal and interest at 10% interest over 15 years

What if I Have to Renovate Immediately?

Sometimes property investors purchase a property that needs "touching up" immediately — the carpet is a bit worn, the inside needs a paint, and the property could do with a carport. These investors are then faced with the dilemma of whether or not to attend to these things straight away.

I believe that if a property needs a few things doing to it, then it should be done immediately. From a taxation viewpoint, it would be unwise to hold off in the hope that the "repairs" might become tax deductible later. The Tax Office would deem that the repairs, even though carried out many years later, were bringing the property back to a condition that was *better* than when it was purchased, not the *same* condition. In such a case, the "repairs" would be "improvements" and could not be claimed as a repair.

Let's look at a situation where $10,000 worth of renovations are carried out soon after a property is purchased. Suppose the renovations were:

Carpet, Curtains, Hot Water System	=	$5,000
Painting, Rubbish Removal	=	$3,000
Carport, Concrete Pad	=	$2,000
Total Cost	=	**$10,000**

Let's look at the overall effect of these renovations in the spreadsheet on the opposite page. The total renovation cost of $10,000 can be added into the loan and is reflected in both the property value (now $150,000) and the increased loan (now $156,000). The interest on the additional loan can be claimed immediately. If, as a result of renovations, the rent was increased to $185 per week, the returns from this investment are unchanged at 36.79%, and likewise the cost per week is the same at $47. Why?

First, we need to distinguish between "repairs" and "capital items". While "repairs" such as painting cannot be immediately claimed as a tax deduction, capital items such as carpets and curtains can be depreciated immediately. In this case, the carpet, curtains, etc. are considered to be "capital items" and could be depreciated, as could the new carport that would qualify for the capital allowance of 2.5%. However, the "repairs" such as painting and rubbish removal could not be claimed for at all.

In effect the increased rent, and the increased tax refund brought about by the extra interest deduction and depreciation claims, offset the additional cost of borrowing the money to carry out the renovations.

You might well ask that if the cost of renovations makes no difference at all to the return, why bother to renovate? Very simply, if you don't renovate when the property needs it there would be a good chance that you would have to drop the rent substantially just to get a tenant!

What if I Have to Renovate Immediately?

Assumptions		Projected results over	5 yrs	10 yrs
Property value	$150,000	Property value	$215,344	$309,155
Deposit	$0	Equity	$59,344	$153,155
Rent per week	$185	After-tax return /yr	69.56%	36.79%
Cap. growth rate	7.50%	IF SOLD		
Inflation rate	5.00%	Selling costs & CGT	$12,188	$33,238
Interest rate	10.00%	Equity	$47,156	$119,917
Marginal tax rate	44.40%	After-tax return /yr	60.25%	32.40%

COMPUTER PROJECTIONS OVER 10 YEARS

ASSUMPTIONS	Inputs	1yr	2yr	3yr	5yr	10yr
Property value	150,000	161,250	173,344	186,345	215,344	309,155
Purchase costs	4,000					
Deposit	0					
Loan	156,000	156,000	156,000	156,000	156,000	156,000
Equity	-6,000	5,250	17,344	30,345	59,344	153,155
Capital growth	7.50%	7.50%	7.50%	7.50%	7.50%	7.50%
Inflation rate	5.00%	5.00%	5.00%	5.00%	5.00%	5.00%
GROSS RENT /wk,/yr	185	9,620	10,101	10,606	11,693	14,924
CASH DEDUCTIONS						
Loan interest I/O	10.00%	15,600	15,600	15,600	15,600	15,600
Property expenses	24.32%	2,340	2,457	2,580	2,844	3,630
PRE-TAX CASH FLOW	0	-8,320	-7,956	-7,574	-6,751	-4,306
NON-CASH DEDUCTIONS						
Deprec.-building	2.50%	2,050	2,050	2,050	2,050	2,050
Deprec.-fittings	15,300	4,050	2,813	2,109	1,187	282
Borrowing costs	2,000	400	400	400	400	
TOTAL DEDUCTIONS	0	24,440	23,320	22,739	22,081	21,562
TAX CREDIT (actual)	44.40%	5,876	5,512	5,340	4,800	3,213
AFTER-TAX CASH FLOW	0	-2,444	-2,444	-2,234	-1,951	-1,093
RATE OF RETURN -IRR	36.79%	———————— Your Cost Per Week ————————				
Before-tax return	66.17%	47	47	43	38	21

Variables Changed from Basic Spreadsheet on page 162:

Rent = $185; Renovations = $10,000

What if my Tax Return Shows a Negative Income?

Some property investors become alarmed when their tax return shows a very low or even negative income, believing that they are over committed on investment property loans. After all, a negative income must surely indicate a precarious financial situation. Indeed, financial institutions also have trouble coming to grips with the very low income levels reflected in the tax returns presented by investors seeking additional loans. Let's look at how this comes about so that you will understand the difference between "taxable income" and "real income" and why there is no need for concern.

Suppose that an investor on $45,000 per year purchases four of the example $140,000 investment properties. The spreadsheet on the opposite page shows the complete set of figures depicting this situation. The value of the property is now $560,000 (4 times $140,000), and most of the other variables such as loan interest, purchasing and borrowing costs are in multiples of four times the basic spreadsheet shown on page 162, with a few notable exceptions.

The tax refund at $12,582 is not four times the tax refund of $5,154 for just one property, because of the graduated tax scales and the fact that the tax refund on the additional deductions is calculated at a lower tax rate. Consequently, the real cost to the investor at $341 per week is also not four times the cost of one property at $47 per week. If the total rent and total deductions in the first year are isolated, then the investor's tax return would look something like this:

Tax Return with Four Rental Properties

Income		Deductions	
Salaried Income	$45,000	Cash Deductions	$67,760
Rental Income	$37,440	Non-cash Deductions	$20,800
Total Income	**$82,440**	**Total Deductions**	**$88,560**
Taxable Income	**-$6,120**	**Tax Payable**	**0**

The total rental income from the four properties at $37,440, added to a salary of $45,000 would produce a total income of $82,440 and the total deductions would be $88,560 (4 times $22,140). The investor's taxable income would be negative at -$6,120 ($82,440 - $88,560) and as a result, he would pay no tax. The losses could even be accrued to the following year. Let's now look at our investor's "real" income, so that you will see that although his tax return shows a negative income, he is NOT destitute and that there is a "missing factor".

What if my Tax Return Shows a Negative Income?

Assumptions		Projected results over	5 yrs	10 yrs
Property value	$560,000	Property value	$803,953	$1.154m
Deposit	$0	Equity	$219,953	$570,178
Rent per week	$720	After-tax return /yr	44.84%	28.39%
Cap. growth rate	7.50%	IF SOLD		
Inflation rate	5.00%	Selling costs & CGT	$38,107	$121,856
Interest rate	10.00%	Equity	$181,845	$448,323
Marginal tax rate	44.40%	After-tax return /yr	37.79%	24.39%

COMPUTER PROJECTIONS OVER 10 YEARS

ASSUMPTIONS	Inputs	1yr	2yr	3yr	5yr	10yr
Property value	560,000	602,000	647,150	695,686	803,953	1.154m
Purchase costs	16,000					
Deposit	0					
Loan	584,000	584,000	584,000	584,000	584,000	584,000
Equity	-24,000	18,000	63,150	111,686	219,953	570,178
Capital growth	7.50%	7.50%	7.50%	7.50%	7.50%	7.50%
Inflation rate	5.00%	5.00%	5.00%	5.00%	5.00%	5.00%
GROSS RENT /wk,/yr	720	37,440	39,312	41,278	45,509	58,082
CASH DEDUCTIONS						
Loan interest I/O	10.00%	58,400	58,400	58,400	58,400	58,400
Property expenses	25.00%	9,360	9,828	10,319	11,377	14,520
PRE-TAX CASH FLOW	0	-30,320	-28,916	-27,442	-24,269	-14,839
NON-CASH DEDUCTIONS						
Deprec.-building	2.50%	8,000	8,000	8,000	8,000	8,000
Deprec.-fittings	41,200	11,200	7,500	5,625	3,164	751
Borrowing costs	8,000	1,600	1,600	1,600	1,600	
TOTAL DEDUCTIONS	0	88,560	85,328	83,944	82,541	81,671
TAX CREDIT (actual)	44.40%	12,582	13,581	14,321	14,376	11,266
AFTER-TAX CASH FLOW	0	-17,738	-15,335	-13,121	-9,893	-3,573
RATE OF RETURN -IRR	28.39%	——————— Your Cost Per Week ———————				
Before-tax return	51.06%	341	295	252	190	69

Variables Changed from Basic Spreadsheet on page 162:

All figures associated with 4 Properties each worth $140,000

The table below shows the investor's "real" income, taking account of his "hip pocket" expenses of just the loan payment and property expenses.

Income/Expenditure with Four Rental Properties

Income		Expenditure	
Salaried Income	$45,000	Loan Payment	$58,400
Rental Income	$37,440	Property Expenses	$9,360
Total Income	$82,440	Total Expenses	$67,760
NET INCOME	=	$82,440 - $67,760 = $14,680	

The total income including salary and rent would be $82,440 and the total expenditure including loan payments (in this case interest only) and property expenses would be $67,760, leaving a net income of $14,680 for living expenses. What's missing? Why doesn't the investor's "real" income of $14,680 match his taxable income of - $6,120? Why is there a discrepancy of $20,800 (the difference between $14,680 and - $6,120)?

The missing factor is the amount of non-cash deductions that are an integral part of the tax return, but do not constitute a real expense. In the model, the missing $20,800 is the sum of all the non-cash deductions, which include the depreciation allowance (or capital allowance) of $8,000, depreciation on the fixtures and fittings at $11,200 and borrowing costs claim of $1,600! Obviously, this investor would not be eating "off the floor" as his tax return suggests, but "on the floor" — courtesy of the non-cash deductions such as the depreciation on the carpet.

Few people fully comprehend the huge impact that these non-cash deductions make and certainly many financiers misinterpret the situation completely.

There have been many instances where the use of "taxable income" as opposed to "real income" has caused a misleading appraisement of an investor's true financial situation. In one particular instance brought to my attention, a company that was entitled to a Research and Development allowance of 150% on labour and equipment was rejected for a loan on the basis that the company profits, as per the taxable income, were zero, when in fact the "real" company profits were several hundreds of thousands of dollars.

Never underestimate the power of "non-cash" deductions to reduce taxable income. When you do your own sums, explain these forgotten sweeteners to your financier, as it can make all the difference between getting and not getting a loan.

Some of the Many "What Ifs" You Can Answer for Yourself by Using our Computer Program

What if I have to lower the rent to get a tenant?

What if the loan has a higher interest rate but lower establishment fee?

What if the property is new?

What if I buy a very old house?

What if I buy a unit instead of a house?

What if I do the conveyancing myself?

What if I use an agent to manage the property?

What if I only earn $20,000 per year?

What if I decide to buy more than one property?

What if rents stagnate for a few years?

What if capital growth is different in each year?

What if I have a rental guarantee for two years?

What if I put in a larger deposit?

What if I pay cash for the property and the extra costs?

What if I borrow the borrowing costs and purchasing costs?

What if I buy a very low yielding property?

What if I sell the property in five years time?

What if the property drops in value after two years?

What if rents drop after two years?

What if I have to add a garage?

What if I take a 15 year P & I loan instead of a 25 year loan?

What if I do the repairs myself?

What if I let the property furnished?

What if inflation is equal to capital growth?

What if the establishment fees are high?

What if the yield is high?

What if I buy an undervalued property?

What if a flat rate of tax is introduced?

What if I buy a commercial property?

What if I bought a property qualifying for a 4% capital allowance?

What if I take an interest-only loan over two years?

What if the body corporate fees are high?

About the publisher...

Somerset Financial Services Pty Ltd[*] specialises solely in residential investment property. Its role is one of research, analysis and education. Formed in 1989, its aim is to provide investors with enough basic information to help them to confidently invest in property. The company does not sell property, finance, or even personal advice. Instead, through seminars, books, videos and computer software, it provides investors with all the objective, independent, well-researched information and tools that they will need to be self sufficient in their investment decisions.

Building Wealth in Changing Times is the third book produced and published by Somerset Financial Services Pty Ltd. The first book *Manual for Residential Property Investors* was reprinted three times in Australia and twice in New Zealand. The Australian version of this manual was replaced in 1992 by the more comprehensive book, *Building Wealth through Investment Property*, which became somewhat of a bible to the thousands of people venturing into residential investment property.

Other products available

Book *Building Wealth through Investment Property*

This book should be the first investment that any potential property investor makes. It has been described as an "authoritative, thoroughly-researched 190 pages of easy-to-read common sense, but a book that may very well change your life". The book has been extremely well received by people from all walks of life, with more than 100,000 copies sold. The book's meticulous step-by-step guide of why and how to invest directly in residential property was distilled from a mountain of information obtained from such institutions as the National and State Real Estate Institutes, BIS Shrapnel, Residex, the Australian Bureau of Statistics, and the Australian Stock Exchange. It also incorporates a wealth of experience gleaned from the author's 20 years of investing in residential property. This invaluable reference book covers everything from a list of typical tax deductions for rental properties, to how to arrange finance and what to look for in an investment property, to a guide for identifying the best source of finance.

Video *Building Your Wealth through Investment Property*

This 75 minute video is based on the seminars presented by Jan Somers. Although it covers much of the same material contained in her books, it is not a substitute for them. Rather, it brings the information in the books to life, providing a broad overview of the why's and how's of investment property, negative gearing, taxation, and finance.

[*] Somerset Financial Services Pty Ltd (ACN 058 152 337)

Computer Programs *PIA (Property Investment Analysis)*

The company's PIA computer program was developed to help people answer their own "what ifs" about property investment and has been described by computer editor Peter Layton as:

Brilliant, logical, and so simple you have to wonder why nobody thought of it before.

The PIA program comes in two versions, one for investors, and one for professionals wishing to assist clients. Both are available for either IBM compatible or Macintosh personal computers. The PIA programs are both very powerful, yet very easy to use.

PIA Advanced Personal

The PIA Advanced Personal program was designed specifically for property investors to help them calculate capital growth, cash flows and rates of return (IRR) on investment properties, taking into account the tax implications in their own personal situation. Apart from answering all their "what ifs", it will help them work out their own specific investment capacity and budget. And once the investment decision has been made, the program can be used to prepare the appropriate detailed financial report for the accountant and bank manager.

The program will compute cash flow projections for up to 40 years and has the facility for changing more than 50 variables including property price, rent, capital growth, inflation, deposit, etc. There is extensive on-line help with more than 50 simplified auxiliary data-entry screens, where the variables can be broken down into their individual components. It is possible to compare the effect of interest-only versus principal and interest loan types and to examine the tax benefits of buying the property in single and joint names. There is also a provision for saving files, and there is the capacity to reset stamp duties and tax scales should the need arise.

PIA Professional

PIA Professional was designed for professionals such as accountants, real estate agents and financiers to enable them to demonstrate the financial aspects of property to investors. In addition to all the features of the Advanced Personal version, it has extensive graphics screens (such as bar charts for debt vs property value), facilities for recording investor's details and a host of other utilities for helping investors understand the benefits of property investment. This program is part of a package which includes the two *Building Wealth* books and the video. It also includes a site licence which enables the program to be used on more than one computer within the one office.

ORDER FORM

PLEASE SEND ME :

Computer Program: *PIA Advanced Personal* $129 [   ]

                         PIA Professional $475 [   ]

DISK SIZE: 5.25" [   ]   3.5" [   ]   *VERSION:* Mac [   ] DOS [   ]

Book: *Building Wealth in Changing Times* $29 [   ]

Book: *Building Wealth through Investment Property* $29 [   ]

Video: *Building Your Wealth through Investment Property* $49 [   ]

TOTAL AMOUNT   [$]

(All Prices Include Postage & Handling)

PLEASE NOTIFY ME:

We are continually producing and updating software and other
material relating to property investment. If you want to be
informed of any new or updated material, please tick the box.   [   ]

Mr/Mrs/Ms_____ First Name _____

Surname _____

Address_____

_____

_____ State _____ P'code _____

Phone No. _____ I enclose a cheque [   ] or please

Debit my Bank Card [   ] Master Card [   ] Visa Card [   ] for $ _____

No |__|__|__|__||__|__|__|__||__|__|__|__||__|__|__|__| Exp __ / __

Card Holder's Signature _____

Please post, phone or fax your order to:

Somerset Financial Services Pty Ltd   Telephone   (07) 286 4368
P.O. Box 615, Cleveland Qld. 4163.   Fax: (07) 821 2005

(To preserve the quality of this book, the order form may be photocopied)